NEW VOICES
FROM THE
LONGHOUSE

NEW VOICES

FROM THE

LONGHOUSE

An Anthology of Contemporary Iroquois Writing

EDITED BY JOSEPH BRUCHAC

Contributing Editors:
Maurice Kenny
Karoniaktatie

The Greenfield Review Press
Greenfield Center, New York

Publication of this anthology has been made possible, in part, through a Literary Publishing Grant from the Literature Program of the New York State Council on the Arts.

ISBN 0-912678-68-2

Library of Congress #87-80178

FIRST EDITION

Composition by Sans Serif, Ann Arbor, MI 48104
Printed in the United States of America.

Cover Art by Richard Hill

CONTENTS

Roberta Hill Whiteman (Oneida)

Ted C. Williams (Tuscarora)

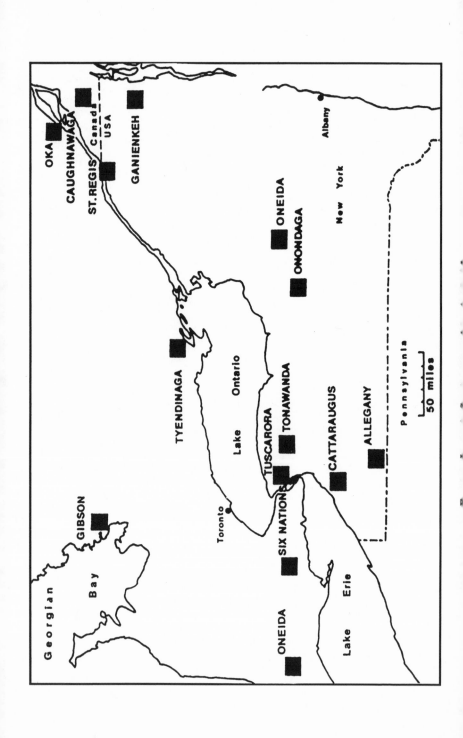

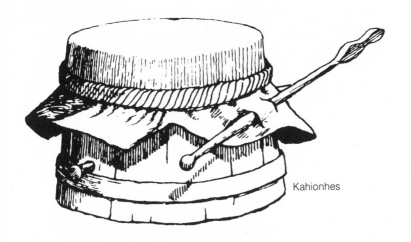

Kahionhes

David Back

My transition into awareness brought forth this immense appreciation for those who have retained the teachings of our ancestors, for
the writings and music that combine into song are only a different
way to say what has been said by the indigenous people of the Americas since the teachings evolved.

It is with these avenues of communication that one may continue
the traditions within these so called modern times, so that the generations to come will also be aware and grateful for their grandfathers as
ours were for theirs.

The Natural Place

The snipe on the shoreline looked up just in time
To greet the one looking for some peace in his mind
Said you've got to slow down your pace
Let the worry go from your face
And welcome to this natural place

The howl of the wolf came before he appeared
And with the four winds he defused all the fears
Singing his old favorite songs
Said this is where you belong
Into the great light of the sun

The bear on the hill top pointed up to the skies
And gave the young visitor some sparkle in his eyes
Giving him the strength to go on
Said now seek the one in the pond
Your vision has found a new dawn

The turtle came afloat and he shared all he knew
Said nothing's more sacred than the natural truth
Then writing in the ivory sand
The message that I now understand
Welcome to the natural land

The Realization

He's running down the hill with his lance in hand
Said to himself, he's gonna die like a man
He felt the sharp pain go straight through his heart
And saw his whole life falling apart
    But when he opened his eyes, he knew he wasn't
        gonna die
    And as he looked to the skies, he saw the reason why
        Ah, how can it be true?
        Ah, how can it be true?
        That we all must die, inside,
        Just to be purified
So with each new dawn of the rising sun
We give thanks that a new life has begun
And just like the warrior fallen in war
Only the Creator knows what's in store
    Yet when he opened his eyes, he knew he wasn't
        gonna die
    And as he looked to the skies, he saw the reason why
        Ah, how can it be true?
        Ah, how can it be true?
        That we all must die, inside,
        Just to be purified

David Back　3

The Holy Man

I heard that the eagle alive
And the holy man he go walking down by the
    riverside
I heard that the culture survived
So the holy man he go walking down by the riverside
— Yet nobody seems to question why
  No, no, nobody seems to question why
I guess in time, in your mind
In your mind, the time will come, by and by
I heard what the medicine say
And the holy man he go walking down by the
    riverside
I heard of the power he pray
And the holy man he go walking down by the
    riverside
I heard of the part that he play
And the holy man he go walking down by the
    riverside
I heard that it is of today
So the holy man he go walking down by the riverside
— Yet nobody seems to question why
  No, no, nobody seems to question why
I guess in time, in your mind
In your mind, the time will come, by and by

Where the River Flows

Said I asked the man, where do our people go?
He say man, we go down where the river flows
Said I asked the man, what do the eagle know?
He say man, we go down where the river flows

    Down there, we'll find the reasons
    Down there, we'll join the seasons
    And so we listen for the drum
    And dance our way into the sun
    Then give thanks for the day that is done
    And together again we ride as one

Said I asked the man, have you seen justice?
He say man, we go down where the river flows
Said I asked the man, is the culture lost as well?
He say man, we go down where the river flows

    Down there, we'll find the reasons
    Down there, we'll join the seasons
    And so we listen for the drum
    And dance our way into the sun
    Then give thanks for the day that is done
    And together again we ride as one

Said I asked the man, d'you see our paths clear?
He say man, we go down where the river flows
Said I asked the man, is the native's day near?
He say man, we go down where the river flows

    Down there, we'll find the reasons
    Down there, we'll join the seasons
    And so we listen for the drum
    And dance our way into the sun

Then give thanks for the day that is done
And together again we ride as one

Said I asked the man, where do our people go?
He say man, we go down where the river flows
Said I asked the man, what do the eagle know?
He say man, we go down where the river flows

Down there, we'll find the reasons
Down there, we'll join the seasons
And so we listen for the drum
And dance our way into the sun
Then give thanks for the day that is done
And together again we ride as one

Salli Benedict

Salli M. Kawennotakie Benedict is a Mohawk of the Wolf clan, who resides on an island in the St. Lawrence River within the territories of the Akwesasne and the Mohawk Nation.

Salli Benedict is the mother of two children, Luz Teiohontasen and Jasmine Kahentineshen, who like to climb tall people.

Old man,
the ancient tremolo
rises from your throat
and I know your heart.
In your voice
I hear too
the messages
that you saved for me,
from those
you have known.
They are carried
in your voice
like distant thunder.
Allow us to hear
more thunder.
Let it echo
for all time.

The Tsioneskwenrie* Plant People

It was springtime, and the woods were alive with new plant life. Many birds had returned to their summer homes.

On the edge of the woods, there lived an old man and his wife. The man was a believer in the curative powers of plant medicines. He used his generous woods to supply him with medicinal needs to keep his wife and himself in good health.

All was not well for him this spring. He was sick in bed from an illness that he had never had before. He sent his wife to the woods several times to get medicines. She would steep a tea from these and give them to her ailing husband to drink. None of them made him better. He grew sicker each day.

Finally, he lapsed into a dream-like sleep. In his dream-sleep, he was in bed and through the door walked a little old man and a little old lady. They had purplish-red skin and shiny white hair. When they came to the side of his bed, he saw that they were not even tall enough to see over the side of his bed. They looked very cheerful. Their round faces glowed and their eyes sparkled.

They said to him, "We are Tsioneskwenrie . . . The Spirit of the plant called Tsioneskwenrie."

They told him that a tea from the purplish-red root of their plant would make him well. Then they told what the plant looked like. It was a short plant with broad leaves and a thick stem. The roots were the same color as they were. They told him that they grew in the shady areas of the woods.

Then the man woke up and told his wife of the dream. His wife went to the woods and found the plant that he described and made a tea for her husband.

The Tsioneskwenrie tea had good results, just as his

---

*The Mohawk word for *wild ginger.*

tiny visitors had promised. The man went out to the woods with his sacred tobacco and his pipe, to give thanks to the Great Spirit for sending the Tsioneskwenrie people to him. He left an offering at the base of a Tsioneskwenrie plant to give thanks to them for their help.

The next day the man felt so good that he went hunting. The man's wife thought that it was such a wonderful medicine that she went to the woods and collected more of the root, and stored them away in a covered jar. When her husband came back from hunting, he was having trouble breathing, and he was feeling very ill. He went to bed. He then fell into another dream-sleep. In his dream he saw the little old man and the little old woman come into the room to the side of his bed to talk to him. He saw that they too were having trouble breathing. Their once bright purplish-red faces were grey, and their once happy faces were sad.

He said, gasping for air as he talked, "Why are your faces so grey, little Tsioneskwenrie people?"

They replied, also gasping for air, "We are having trouble breathing because your wife has put the Tsioneskwenrie root in a jar and covered it. Our spirit needs air to breathe, just as you do. Take the roots from the jar and put them in a burlap bag, and hang it outside in your shed. The burlap will allow the air to get to the roots, so that we can breathe."

When he awoke from his dream-sleep, he rushed to the shelf and opened the jar. His breathlessness was eased. He found a burlap bag and placed the Tsioneskwenrie roots in it, and hung it in his shed.

The next morning when he had recovered, he went to the woods to give thanks to both the Great Spirit and his helpers the Tsioneskwenrie people.

Tahotahontanekentseratkerontakwenhakie

Deep in the woods, there lived a man and his wife, and their newborn baby boy. The baby was so young that his parents had not yet given him a name. Hunting was very bad that winter and they had very little to eat. They were very poor.

One day around suppertime, a little old man came to their door. He was selling rabbits.

"Do you wish to buy a rabbit for your supper?" he asked.

The woman who met him at the door replied that they were very poor and had no money to buy anything.

It was growing dark and the man looked very tired. The woman knew that he had travelled very far just to see if they would buy a rabbit from him. She invited him to stay for supper and share what little they had to eat.

"What is your name?" the husband asked as he got up to meet the old man.

"I have no name," the little man replied. "My parents were lost before they could name me. People just call me Tahotahontanekentseratkerontakwenhakie which means, 'He came and sold rabbits.' "

The husband laughed. "My son has not been named yet either. We just call him The Baby."

The old man said, "You should name him so that he will know who he is. There is great importance in a name." The old man continued, "I will give you this last rabbit of mine for a good supper, so that we may feast in honor of the birth of your new son."

In the morning, the old man left. The parents of the baby still pondered over a name for the baby.

"We shall name the baby after the generous old man who gave him a feast in honor of his birth. But he has no name," the mother said.

"Still, we must honor his gift to our son," the husband replied. "We will name our son after what people call the old man, Tahotahontanekentseratkerontakwenhakie which means, 'He came and sold rabbits.' "

"What a long name that is," the mother said. "Still, we must honor the old man's wish for a name for our son and his feast for our son."

So the baby's name became Tahotahontanekentseratkerontakwenhakie which means, "He came and sold rabbits," in honor of the old man.

The baby boy grew older and became very smart. He had to be, to be able to remember his own name. Like all other children he was always trying to avoid work. He discovered that by the time his mother had finished calling his name for chores, he could be far, far away.

Sometimes his mother would begin telling him something to do, "Tahotahontanekentseratkerontakwenhakie . . . hmmmm . . . " She would forget what she wanted to have him do, so she would smile and tell him to go and play.

Having such a long important name had its disadvantages too. When his family travelled to other settlements to visit friends and other children, the other children would leave him out of games. They would not call him to play or catch ball. They said that it took more energy to say his name than it did to play the games.

News of this long, strange name travelled to the ears of the old man, Tahotahontanekentseratkerontakwenhakie. "What a burden this name must be for a child," the old man thought. "This name came in gratitude for my feast for the birth of the boy. I must return to visit them."

The old man travelled far to the family of his namesake, Tahotahontanekentseratkerontakwenhakie. The parents met the old man at the door and invited him in. He brought with him food for another fine meal.

"You are very gracious to honor me with this namesake," he said. "But we should not have two people wandering this world, at the same time, with the same name. People will get us confused, and it may spoil my business. Let us call your son Oiasosonaion which means, 'He has another name.' If people wish to know his other name, then he can tell them."

Oiasosonaion smiled and said, "I will now have to call you Tahotahontanekentseratkerontakwenhakie tanon Oiasahosonnon which means, 'He came and sold rabbits and gave the boy another name.' "

Everyone laughed.

Sweet Grass Is Around Her

A woman was sitting
on a rock.
I could see her
clearly,
even though
she was far away.
She was Teiohontasen,
my mother's aunt.
She was a
basket maker.
When I was young,
my mother told me
that her name meant,
"Sweetgrass is all around her."
I thought that it was a good name
for a basket maker.
She was in her eighties
now.
She was short like me,
and a bit stout.
She knew the land well;
and the plants,
and the medicines,
and the seasons.
She knew how to talk
to the Creator too;
and the thunderers,
and the rainmakers.
She had a big bundle of sweetgrass
at her side.
It was long, and green,
and shiny.
Her big straw hat

shaded
her round face.
It was very hot.
She pulled her mid-calf-length dress
down to her ankles,
over her rubber boots.
She brought her lunch
in a paper bag;
a canning jar of cold tea,
fried bread,
sliced meat,
and some butter,
wrapped in tin foil.
She placed them carefully
on the rock.
She reached
into the bag,
and pulled out a
can of soft drink.
I thought it strange.
She didn't drink
soft drinks.
Then,
she reached for her
pocket knife.
Basket makers always
have a good knife.
It was in the pocket of
the full-length
canvas apron,
that was always
safety-pinned to her dress.
She made two sandwiches,
  . . . looked around
Saw me looking at her.
Her eyes sparkled,
she smiled.
She lifted up the soft drink,

and signaled me to come.
After we ate,
she stood up
on the rock
and looked out.
She smelled the air.
I knew that she
could smell the sweetgrass.
I never could.
She pointed to
very swampy land.
Mosquitoes, I thought.
I was dressed poorly.
We didn't talk much
but we could hear,
and listen to each other.
She never forced me
to speak Mohawk.
Mohawk with an
English accent
made her laugh.
She didn't
want to hear English though.
We would spend
all day
picking sweetgrass.
Sometimes
we would look for
medicines.
One time,
my mother asked her
what she thought
Heaven would be like.
She said
that there was sweetgrass everywhere
and people made
the most beautiful
baskets.

Peter Blue Cloud / Aroniawenrate

Turtle Clan, Mohawk (Ganienkehaka) Nation at Kahnawake (within Quebec, so-called).

Has edited assorted journals and magazines since 1969.

Five books published are out of print. Sixth is *Sketches In Winter, With Crows* – Strawberry Press.

Elderberry Flute Song (Contemporary Coyote Tales) reprinted by White Pine Institute.

Winter Crow

I awakened to diffused light. A frost painting upon the window was subtly lit by a full moon high above. Ferns and giant trees tossed and swayed in a silent wind storm. It was neither night nor day, but a half sleeping landscape.

Three hunters walked through the trees. The trees had become pines, tightly twisted small ancients in a land of lakes and muskeg. The hunters were lost. And because true silence is the muted sound of everything in Creation, I heard a large, flat, hand-held drum. The moon was a polished disc of shell. Voices came to me from afar. As if from over hills and through a passage known only to themselves, the voices reached for me.

It is yesterday, I thought to myself, pulling the quilt closer around my shoulders. Lying here in bed staring at a window, I entered time without knowing how. I slowly dissolved into particles of vapor, the moon letting me become partly a shaft of vague light slanting through a window.

The hunters passed me without acknowledging my presence. I did not exist in their world. They held between themselves an invisible hunger of a people, the spirit of that hunger so powerful in its plea that all else was as nothing. I was given visions of starving children and elders on the steam of the hunters' breaths. I drew the scattered self of me back together to become a power of warmth in the breasts of these hunters. The horned four-leggeds would await their coming. There would be a lean feast of what winter had left. The children and elders would grease their lips and line their stomachs with a lean fat. This was my only wish.

I touched the frosted landscape of my windowpane and left a huge dark bird etched there. Winter's Crow was brother to the moon. He followed the hunters of a people in silence, he was concerned for the hunters. He saw far ahead of them what they sought and gave to them the vision I had borrowed from Creation. Each of us, Crow and myself, were content in our present meaning.

Again the singing voices reached for me. They are all my yesterdays, I thought again. And Crow, whom I had not known was part of this other thinking, "gra-awed" me my self-centered echo and gave me a portrait of an ego lying frozen in the snow. He grawed again to wake the sleeping dream of tomorrow and lent me, momentarily, a portion of my own reasoning. Then I heard again the voices which were indeed tomorrow. They were seven voices. They were spaced across a landscape in seven generations in time. Then, as their voices faded, I heard their echoes behind me and turned to confront another landscape. And these, too, were spaced across a landscape in seven generations going back into time. And I stood in the center of these and knew, yes knew, that if I were to approach the future singers, the first would merge into me and another seventh would appear far ahead. And if I approached the past singers, they too would merge my body and create another seventh back in time, perhaps beyond my puny vision.

Again Crow grawed. Again I reached to finger-etch another Crow, knowing that crows travel in pairs, one the shadow self of the other. They landed upon a bare winter branch above my head and began telling me stories of times past and times to come. I will write all of these stories to share with you as they occur to me.

In the meantime these crows again grawed me deeply with belly-born rumblings which became woodstove sputterings. And so I again pulled the quilt closer yet and just before I entered another dream, I saw the frozen landscape upon the window transform into a soft eagerness of youthful plants about to emerge from soil.

An ancient couple bent to slowly hoe green rows of corn. I drew near to them, near enough to peer into their eyes and faces. And what I saw was myself with crooked, yellow teeth, content in the rhythm of the hoe. And the one who worked by my side was my grandmother, her ancient, sparse white hair gathered-up in a blue kerchief.

Again Crow grawed, and I awoke to morning.

18

A Gentle Earthquake

(for Mt. St. Helens)

An all night summer wind, hot — Once
and dry without a hint of seas. — a
A restless tossing, turning series — feast
of short-lived dreams set mind — was
to rhythms of remembered oceans. — given
A rolling shiver of earth skin — and
shakes the vessel of this sleeping house, — every-
and caught between dream and awakening — one
I wait for the next slight tremor. — ate.

Mama Coyote and her two pups — Once
respond to the earthquake in song — a
as if having known and sat the night — song
awaiting their cue, and a bird, too, — was
cheeps a short, shrill, many-sided — sung
note, joining the keening barks. — in
The dry, brown grasses bend to — praise
the slight increase in wind, as — of
crickets one by one begin again — all.

their chorus of song. (And if restless, — Once
you may, like me, untangle yourself — a
from twisted sheets to dress in darkness — drum
and in darkness go outdoors to stand — was
and breathe of grass-scented wind — pulse
and raise face to sky and suck — to
in breath, astonished that such — the
a vast and brilliant display of — all-
stars keep happening into eternity.) — ness.

Quickly forgotten dreams, dropped to — Once
earth, as star fingers which are — a
thoughts, pluck nerve ends to — people
further expand the universal wheel, — lived
and the crickets, too, rejoice and — in
grow their song among invisible — balance

grasses which are seas which
reflect the song in star pictures
floating upon an endless ocean.

An earthquake is not a devastation,
a malicious act of nature against man.
An earthquake is because it must be.
The early morning newsperson reports
minor damage here and there. He does
not declare a state of emergency. He
does not suggest a praise to earth
her wonderous breath of life

so freely given. Yes, ah, yes, it
takes humanity, pencil, and paper,
to sit as I commenting on events. Now,
this short time later, I fashion
a parchment of green oak leaves
against a blue sky, take up
a brush of soaproot buried deep,
and for pigment mix my sweat

with tobacco juice left by grasshopper,
white foam spit of frog, cupped
dewdrops from varied flowers,
a touch of robin "cheer-up",
a faint trace of coyote barkings,
and mix this delicate pigment
in the hollow vessel of a concave
thought, and begin to paint

a landscape/dreamscape/
futurescape/mindscape, dwelling
on cloud-thoughts soon to be
evaporated over countless seas:
ribs of rainbows, skulls of boulders
strewn over a granite base of
bedrock reflecting glaciers
given once in yesterday.

I sit upon a stone hill, a mile
above a green and winding river.

with
Crea-
tion.

The
sky
is
a
feast
of
stars
which

are
drum
beats
in
a
song
return-
ing.

A
rattle
is
an
earth-
quake
shak-
ing.

A
bull-
roarer
is
wind
force
call-
ing.

A
flute

Upon the trail I'd encountered
old cedar posts leaning, some
lying lichen-coated upon leaves.
Small metal tags hammered into
trees proclaim BLM or private

is
all
life
sing-
ing.

ownership. I think of crumbled
villages of stone far to the south,
of cobble pictures in the sand
just across these high sierras.
I suck in breath and pull a drink
from the river far below, trying
to ignore the one-man dredge

Light-
ning
is
masked
dancer
in-
viting

whining its greed as it sucks-up
sand and pebbles searching for gold.
I embarrass myself with a sob
which wracks my body just once,
brought on by mind's fingers
dipping into the away down there
river, and asking again, again:

us
to
join
the
round
dance
night.

Who guards your waters now?
And these beautiful bluffs and
forested hills: who are the guardians,
who, indeed are the guardians of
this good earth? Surely not us!
Guardianship which is Creation's song
no longer issues from our lips.

Fire
is
a
call
to
feast.
Water

Is it possible to shout back the praise
which was given us once in a long ago
yesterday? To dream back the dreamers?
There is a metal tag nailed to my
forehead, and it says, BLM. There is
barbwire wrapped around my wrists.

is
sur-
round-
ing
us
all.

How did it come to be that we
gave over the power of Creation's
balance, to government agencies and
corporations bent on destruction?

The
sen-
tence
of

It is much like sending yourself as
a child, to government boarding school.

The old parchments of law are brittle,
and because they had to be written
down and re-read for enlightenment,
there, under glass, they cannot
even become the compost they
were surely meant to be.

The Great Law of Peace of
the Six Nations is a beginning:
it is a lifeway memorized and
recited to the people. Memory is
knowing, mind is Creation space:
mind is, we are, Creation dreaming.

   The lands of earth are floating plates,
the scientists now say. The Huichol have
a story of Coyote biting turtle and
shattering her shell, and when he
did so, World Pond dried-up, dying.

It took all of the creatures of earth
and the memory of turtle and water
to sing a plea to Coyote to please
regurgitate the allness of turtle,
and when he did so: water was.

Is it greed to call ourselves the
people creatures of turtle island?
Can it be that turtle is still
shattered, and is more than a
continent, more than mere imagination?

An ancient people are those
who remember an original
promise. I meditate upon the
rhythm of a shovel at work,
I ponder the earthworm in wonder.

Volcanic ash is floating to fall
all over earth, covering combustible

a
snake

trail
in
sand,
a
fish
float-

ing
in
its
own
space,
a

bird
sings
us
"ah-
waken."

Seeds
of
corn
fall-
ing,

green
beans
ripen-
ing,
fat

squash
and
melons
tempt-
ing,

rain
fall-

rivers, polluted lakes, nuclear plants,	ing
in a soft blanket of warning.	rain.
An old Hopi is hoeing his cornfield,	Sun
A Mohawk village is surrounded	warm-
by armed troops. A Cree is	ing
spearing fish which will slowly	sun.
poison his own loved family.	Night
On the other side of earth	sleep-
a shaman on a high plateau	ing
is praising the dawn. Her song	night.
stirs the leaves outside my window,	Green
her shadow is a cloud passing by,	sprouts
she is a warm breath of wind	from
which soothes my sleeping children.	earth,
On the other side of earth	tend-
and south, a painted human	er
twirls a bull-roarer and the sound	green.
pauses momentarily, as earth	Hands
searches for her missing nations.	cupped
An eagle wheels the sun.	to
Between two oceans, I hear the	drink
scraping of my grandfather's hoe,	clear
an echo of thirty years returned.	water,
An unborn child whimpers in sleep,	water
a fawn staggers to stand on	emerg-
trembling legs, as ears twitch in	ing
wonder. Again earth skin	from
rolling, nodding stars. Now	ground
the voices murmur close by,	water
all the ancients are returned.	liv-
Our small existence is reflected	ing
on the underbelly of a tortoise,	in

waves of coral light shadows   sky,
in this World Pond, dreaming.   water

A sea of waving grasses   con-

hooves of extinct creatures   tain-

ourselves in exile, and always   ing

a forgiving earth.   Earth.

Friends,

*This poem was composed in a week of early
mornings with day trips to Bald Mt.
An earthquake set me off writing it, with
the eruption of Mt. St. Helens just a while
before.
The visual structure is: seeing it as a long,
single page broadside of the mind. So then,
the words become stories within
stories/some, thoughts as they occurred on
my walks, or thought upon next morning.
The story at right is a staff of mt. lilac,
unpeeled, simple, yet meant to guide. To be
read as a whole after the main body.
It is of course meant to be read aloud.
Since my reading tour I'm much more into
moving my lips, mumbling my early
morning compositions, having experienced
the difference between mind poems on paper,
& aloud poems/or songs.
Maybe it's a wind-dancer, whirly small
tornado funnel, sucking-up loose dust, bits of
paper, scattered memories, etc.?*

San Juan Ridge
Sierra/Nevada Foothills
California

Coyote Speaks of the Myth of Humanity
(Lecture II)

Recorded by Peter Blue Cloud

"You ask about the first humans? It would be more appropriate to ask about the last, perhaps. A short-lived species, they are running at this moment to meet their own extinction. No other creature known to the Creation has the urge to destroy itself as they do. They glory in the destruction of all things and most especially themselves.

"This is the third round and maybe there will never be a fourth. I helped create the first pair far back in time, just after the earth was planted with a greenness of beauty. Along with all the other animal creatures, we decided to try these walking two-leggeds; our plan at the time fit them perfectly into the life balance, an integral part of the allness.

"Hah! Had we but known! Maybe we should have made them to walk about on all fours, thus keeping their eyes more busy at the business of hunting and gathering their sustenance than the upright walking position which acted immediately to make them think themselves above all others. Or perhaps we should have given them long tails to swish about in vanity or vexation in the gathering of burrs and other minor distractions.

"Yes, a pair they were indeed, male and female, meant to multiply and exist within the balance. We gave them hands with fingers capable of making beautiful and useful objects. And more important yet, they were given minds of great expanse to enable them to invent such things as baskets and bowls and, possibly, lovely pictures to delight the eye and imagination.

"And though they were the first of their kind, their thoughts immediately began playing with concepts of incest, self-gratification and greed. They circled one another, sniffing, whining reassurances, each wondering how best to win the other's confidence. Oh, they loved, yes, they loved, but in their loving each looked within itself, asking: is this what I want/desire?

"I was disgusted at what I'd helped fashion. No, I was horrified! Yes, horrified! Imagine what might come to be if these awful creatures should grow and spread their self-centered concepts. So I killed them! Dead. Then I built a fire; no use in wasting good food I thought. And as they cooked I smelled the odors of sweetness. As their fat and flesh sputtered and popped in the fire my mouth watered. Then I noticed another odor, an acrid whiff of something in a thread of yellow smoke mingling the grey. The odor became vile. I retched to it. A tree close by folded its leaves, and though it was the springtime of life, the tree became autumn.

"No, I didn't eat the creatures. There was some element in that acrid smell which entered my brain and was destined to give me my first bad dreams. I went and sat on a small hill waiting for the bodies to be consumed by fire. And when all that remained were powdery ashes, I covered these with soil and stones and quickly left the place.

"Let us try again, we said. Mark those words! We had accepted a challenge without realising it, our adversary our own mistake, or more: that wisp of acrid yellow poisoned smoke had permeated, already, the wondrous new world of the Creation and the seed of doubt, misgiving and other forms of constipation had been firmly planted.

"So, yes, and yes again, we rose (we thought, or, as it were) to the challenge. And in the same image as the first we created another set of two-legged creatures with the very same attributes, except that both were males. Our excuse, or rather our genius, (or maybe our just desserts, but why do I go on fabricating words within or upon words? Get to the meat of it, isn't that what you wish to hear?) decided us that if we were to create two males, thus giving them time to adjust and relax with one another, get to know each other, experiment with life a bit, just maybe, this would act to calm and assure them their proper place within the life balance. Then later, we would create the females.

"Ah, such dreaming. Such manipulations to assuage the ego. Unknowingly (or was it?) yes, I had developed an ego. Yes, without realizing it, I had become Coyote. Vanity, determination and hard-headedness had entered the scene. I can't remember, but perhaps I'd already forgotten my role as helper to the Creation. The humble helper, myself, had become the aggressive, self-appointed knower of truth: 'I will do it right this time!' This I vowed to the Creation. (Yes, I remember now. Creation smiled once before departing to other places and left behind a thought, one which I at the time allowed myself to think my own: Life into life, death into rebirth: that's all, nothing more.)

"And so busy was I, that I paid little attention to the two-legged twins, who by this time were experimenting with clay, painting themselves in over-zealous display. Then they found voice and began making up what they considered to be songs. Yelling and screaming it was, one to the other. And the progression was very swift, from yelling to brandishing rocks and sticks, and even striking at one another in mock battle. But of course mock battling wasn't to satisfy them for very long and they soon fell to the more serious business of slaughter, or murder if you will. And indeed it was strange to see the victor standing over the fallen victim who exactly resembled himself. And no, of course he wasn't satisfied with this singular manifestation of mayhem, but was striding back and forth looking all around, seeking-out his next victim.

"And when I finally came back to myself and noted his treachery, I coughed politely to attract his attention, (thinking to question his motivations, now that I was Coyote: the great arbitrator and creature of wisdom) and he wheeled on me preparing to rush me.

"So yes, I killed him too, without even thinking. For I was by now so wrapped-up in my own importance that little else mattered.

"And without thinking twice I took upon myself to create a new male and female of the species, not as a curiosity, but as a dare to my own genius. Yes, this time I would see to it that they lived within the balance, that they obeyed my rules. Can you imagine that? Obey? Me?

"Yes, I see you all sitting there squirming and casting

hungry eyes at the roundhouse entrance. I know you want to leave, and that you are becoming bored with my recitation, but please, hear me out.

"You must understand that they were like toys, fascinating playthings. I had no idea how it would all turn out. I planned to put them away as soon as I'd finished with them.

"I was summoned to the other side of Creation for consultation. Creation was so polite that it took many, many lifetimes to reach the point: which was that it, Creation, thought that I'd made a very great mistake in re-creating those two-leggeds. I apologized and promised to do away with my errors. 'But no,' Creation said, 'it is too late.'

"So then, we are overrun, as is the rest of the earth. And I apologize to all of you. And I promise you that those two-leggeds will soon be gone again. Left to themselves they have invented bigger and better sticks and stones to do away with one another.

"And when they are gone, I want to assure you and promise, not as Coyote, but as that first helper at the beginning of all things: that it won't happen again. No, it will never happen again, that plague which calls itself Humanity."

The Old Man's Lazy,

I heard the Indian Agent say,
has no pride, no get up
and go. Well, he came out
here and walked around my
place, that agent. Steps
all thru the milkweed and
curing wormwood; tells me
my place is overgrown
and should be made use
of.
   The old split cedar
fence stands at many
angles, and much of it
lies on the ground like
a curving sentence of
stick writing. An old
language, too, black with
age, with different
shades of green of moss
and lichen.
        He always
says he understands us
Indians,
      and why don't
I fix the fence at least:
so I took some fine
hawk feathers fixed
to a miniature woven
shield
    and hung this
from an upright post
near the house.

He
came by last week
and looked all around
again, eyed the feathers
for a long time.
He didn't
say anything, and he didn't
smile even, or look within
himself for the hawk.

Maybe sometime I'll
tell him that the fence
isn't mine to begin with,
but was put up by
the white guy who used
to live next door.
It was
years ago. He built a cabin,
then put up the fence. He
only looked at me once,
after his fence was up,
he nodded at me as if
to show that he knew I
was here, I guess.
It was
a pretty fence, enclosing
that guy, and I felt lucky
to be on the outside
of it.
Well, that guy
dug holes all over his
place, looking for gold,
and I guess
he never
found any. I watched
him grow old for over
twenty years, and bitter,
I could feel his anger
all over the place.

And
that's when I took to
leaving my place to do
a lot of visiting.
                Then
one time I came home
and knew he was gone
for good.

My children would
always ask me why I
didn't move to town
and be closer to them.
    Now, they
tell me I'm lucky to be
living way out here.
                And
they bring their children
and come out and visit me,
and I can feel that they
want to live out here
too, but can't
for some reason, do it.

Each day
a different story is
told me by the fence:
the rain and wind and snow,
the sun and moon shadows,
this wonderful earth,
    this Creation.
I tell my grandchildren
many of these stories,
    perhaps
this too is one of them.

Francis Boots / Ateronhiatakon

My name is Ateronhiatakon. I am Ganienkehaga (Mohawk), from Akwesasne. A student with many interests, most importantly to learn about knowing.

I grew up in a large family, raised with strong cultural and community values and identity. From a very early age I learned about identity, language customs and ways. These ways are hard and sometimes painful. I cherish them all today. It is a gift. What I understand the intent of this gift is that it is to be shared. My interest in stories and teachings goes back beyond memory. It all comes with duty and responsibility, for when one learns of these teachings what is to be done with that knowledge?

I owe a lot to my teachers, for their strength to continue their instructions of nurturing us with wisdom. My friend who helps me discover these gifts in a meaningful way. This is reflected in the oral and written transmission of "Iroquoian use of Wampum". My goal is to continue to learn. In my learning perhaps I can also teach the values I find in the teachings and traditions. I believe that within these ways is strength medicine for all who care to seek its guidance.

Iroquoian Use of Wampum

*On well worn tourist trails, main and back road museums join "made by Indians" traders in describing wampum as "Indian money." However, the use of wampum by the Iroquois as a trade item was of secondary importance at most. Sir William Johnson wrote in 1753, "It is obvious to all who are the least acquainted with Indian affairs, that they regard no message or invitation, be it of what consequence it will, unless attended or confirmed by strings or belts of wampum, which they look upon as we our letters, or rather bonds."**

Onkwehonwe, the original people, have been instructed that, for whatever purpose the people come together, before all else come together, before all else comes the *Ohenten kariwatekwen*, the thoughts which bring our minds together to collectively express our gratitude. We address each other as brothers and sisters of the same creation, as friends and human beings, the way we are instructed to greet one another. We greet each other in peace and goodwill. We say good health to one another, so be it our minds. And the people reply, they will say *to* or *nio*. We give thanks to the earth, the giver of life, to the waters, to the plant life, to all of the animals, the insects and the fish, to the life and forces that are in the sky world, eldest brother sun, grandmother moon, the stars, to the four spiritual beings who guide our people, to Dekanawidah, the Peacemaker, to Ayonwentha, to Skanietariio, Handsome Lake, to Sonkoiatisen, our Creator. We say thank you to Sonkoiatisen for giving us all these things and the continuation of our generations and the assurance that we have this love, that we have this peace, that we have this strength, and that we have this righteousness in our rela-

---

*Letter of Sr. William Johnson, 1753. Doc. Hist. N.Y., vol. ii. p. 624.

tionship with wherever you are listening to our words. So be it our minds.

I want to share the words of the people who are no longer with us, who in their teaching of me intended that I should pass on these words to a younger generation. There are many variations of these teachings, but I am going to share a version that I heard while I was growing up and sitting in the longhouse listening. What I saw that impressed me was the respect and honor that my grandparents would show when they handled *obnikohra*, wampum.

To the *Hodenosaunee*, the Iroquois people, wampum held, and holds, the special significance of a message given through a spiritual means. We are told that wampum was given to us a long time ago by Ayonwentha (Hiawatha), one of the very special men among our Iroquois people, who helped Dekanawidah, the Peacemaker, establish *Kaianerekowa*, the Great Peace, known as the League of the Five Nations or the Iroquois Confederacy. At the time Ayonwentha received these wampums he had lost his daughters. He was in great sadness, and he did not know what to do next. A message came to him as he was walking beside a lake, and in one version of the story a flock of geese came to this lake and picked up the water. On the remaining lake bed lay strings of wampum. Ayonwentha said, "If I ever meet a man who has this same grief, who has this same loss that I am feeling, here is what I would begin to say to him in condolences." He would say to him that life has to continue. Although we acknowledge a great loss in our life, we have to look at the life cycle that will continue. The sun will shine tomorrow, just as it did today. The moon will continue her direction. The Mother Earth will continue her cycles. And so it was that he found the words that are still used for the condolence messages today when our leaders, both men and women, pass away. Ayonwentha, a great statesman, in his grief, found in his heart what he would say to his fellow man who would be in the same condition as himself. The wampum is the evidence of the sincerity of the condolences.

Ohnikohra is made from the quahog shell. The quahog shell has two colors, an area where it is purely white, almost ivory, and areas that are more purplish. Wampum is made from both the ivory and the purplish areas. There are notations as to how the combinations of purple, white, and purple and white beads are strung. It is the significance of how they are strung that the interpreter or orator must remember and recite. This requires considerable insight and training. We say that a man who can do this has a gift given to him by a spiritual power, and that gift belongs to the people. It just flows through the orator: the gift does not belong to him, it is a gift that the people have been given through the orator.

The Mohawk, Onondaga, Seneca, Cayuga, and Oneida nations comprise the [original] Confederacy. Each has a string of wampum beads. We refer to that string of beads as the nation's council fire, and it is a symbol present during councils. A fire is burning, and whatever words we use while this wampum is displayed have to be kind and gentle words. The nation's council fire wampum is brought out for important national, inter-national, and multi-national meetings. It is known and acknowledged by the people that the bearer of this wampum belt represents the nation's one-minded consensus. When he speaks, he speaks with the collective in mind. That means the men elders, the women elders, the chiefs, the clan mothers, the faith keepers, the children, and even the future generations. And so you can perhaps imagine the commitment, the thorough peace, that wampum bearers must find in their own minds when they take wampum in their hands.

There are many, many different types of wampum. The messenger's wampum, for example, would be used for an announcement of a Grand Council (meeting of all nations of the Confederacy) or a nation's meeting. This wampum string is a short one fastened on a wooden stick, and the man who carries it is recognized by the nation. He is given this wampum and a message announcing a meeting. Often there are marks on the stick which indicate in how many days the meeting will be held. He will travel directly to the nation, where he will deliver this message, and only this message. Then he will return immediately to the source which sent the wampum out. The main purpose of the messenger's wampum is to give a specific message about a meeting or an issue which needs to be discussed and relates to the people as a whole.

Wampum is the symbol of the authority that the women hold, and when there is a specific and important message that is to be exchanged, this wampum is brought out. The people will then know that this person is speaking from a particular family [clan] with an urgent message and that all should hear and adhere to the message that is being given.

Wampum historically was used to record agreements between the Hodenosaunee and other nations or governments. For example, when the Hodenosaunee met with the Dutch, they acknowledged each other's existence and developed a relationship. The Hodenosaunee understanding of that relationship is recorded in a belt called the *Kaswenta*. The *Kaswenta* is also known as the Two-Row Wampum belt, and there is a very special meaning for us in that belt, even today. The Two-Row Wampum belt is about 2½ feet long and has two purple parallel lines which run the length of the belt on a white background. This particular belt denotes the type of relationship the nations of the Hodenosaunee expected to have with the Dutch and other arriving nations for all time to come.

The *Kaswenta* represents the continuous flow of life. One purple row signifies the Onkwehonwe. In that row would be the canoe, and in the canoe would be the Onkwehonwe people, their language, their culture, their customs, and their ways. Whatever is important to their understanding of their own identity is there, complete for future generations. However, the Hodenosaunee acknowledged another row, and in that row would be the vessels of other nations, the Dutch in this case. The Dutch had their own language, culture, customs and ways; their past and future are in their vessel.

In their agreement with the Dutch, the Onkwehonwe said to them: we are not your son, we do not have a relationship in which your king will be our father, but rather we are equals and we are brothers; we are created as brothers and we can flow down the river of life, each in our respective vessels and canoe. We can have a relationship, a communication, an understanding about one another, but we are not to steer the other's vessel or canoe. This meant that neither the Dutch nor the Hodenosaunee were to legislate laws or influence in a detrimental way which would re-direct each other's full heritage, language, and culture. The example given is that if anyone crosses from the canoe to the vessel or the vessel to the canoe, there is a concern that there may be rough waters. A wind might come, and if there are people who are straddling these two vessels, there is fear that they might not survive that storm, the people might fall. That message, ancient as it is, has a very important significance today.

There are many, many ways in which the people symbolized words and happenings or future direction through wampum. One of the more common ones, and there are different versions of this, is the *Teiokiokwanhakton*, commonly referred to as the Circle of Unity wampum. This wampum commemorates the establishment of *Kiianorekowa*. The people wanted to remember how important unity is, so they strung two rows of wampum beads and made a circle which has two inter-woven strands. From this circle hang the strings which denote the positions, the authority of *Rotiahneson* and *Iotiahneson*, the Chiefs and Clan Mothers, which is to say the families. In this circle of wampum are the spaced denotations of nationhood. There is a denotation where the strand is much longer. This represents Tadodaho, who is the keeper of the central fire of the Hodenosaunee, Onondaga. The special message in this wampum, we are told, is that there is no issue more important than the peace and unity of the people. We should not allow anything to creep into the minds of the men and women who sit on this council which would be a deterrent or cause destruction to the total unity of the confederacy. The message specifies that each nation has to maintain unity, has to maintain peace, and their responsibility is expressed in words. Words are what we were given, and words are very important. Oratory is an important part of our teachings.

Very regularly, at Six Nations [the Tuscarora nation was given membership in the Confederacy after 1722] meetings what they are doing is taking the wampum belts and stretching them. This means they are making sure the wampum beads are, in fact, intact. At the same time they make sure that someone has the same strength as the leather thongs that hold the beads together. This means the orator's strength, the strength of living life that emanates from the wampum, to be able to speak and present the oratory surrounding the wampum belts, beads, and strings. An old piece of leather, as in nature, deteriorates over a number of years. Parts need to be replaced, fresh thongs are necessary, the belt must be made strong continuously. More importantly, the message that belongs to the belt must be fixed in memory to make sure that someone has that message to hand down.

Always within the wampum message is the interpretation and life experiences are included in the interpretation of these messages. And so the wampum is alive from one generation to the next. Today our wampums are in glass cases in museums throughout the world, and many of our own young people, our own Iroquois people, pass by these glass cases and look at our wampum belts in awe, wondering what they could have been used for because the museum did not include the tradition and the words of the belts in the displays. The wampum belts, beads, and strings are used as reminders for the speaker, but it is the speaker who knows the words. The wampum belts themselves do not speak; one has to know the culture, the language, the words, the feelings, the life around what happened with these wampums in order to understand the real significance, and when wampum belts are in display cases they do not generate that kind of spirituality. Sometimes I think that historians, although they don't mean to, perhaps want to put us in an historical time and they don't allow us to say "but it is alive today." This oratory is here today and we can still hear these things. We know the words today. Historians perhaps want us to say, well it used to be like that. Yes, it used to be like that, but it still is, and it will be for the future, and I believe this.

Rokwaho

Duwayne Leslie Bowen

If we ever meet, call me "Duce." I am of the Seneca People. I reside with my family on the Allegany Indian Reservation at Salamanca, NY. My wife is Janis and my "kitties" are Pam, Guy and 'Chelle. Pam is studying at Fredonia State University, Fredonia, NY and the twins are students at Salamanca High School.

I grew up in the Coldspring/Quaker Bridge area of the reservation. It is no longer in existence; taken by the flood waters of the Kinzua Dam. I miss my home.

Recently our family decided to join the local church. The activity and fellowship is good. There is excellent value in the fellowship.

I have finished a short story. It is a story of an early Iroquoian incident.

Contemporary Seneca Stories of the Supernatural:

Preface

What you are about to read is a result of my interest in the supernatural. I have always been fascinated by stories of the supernatural. I have listened to many people tell of personal experiences of supernatural happenings; I have read numerous books and accounts of supernatural phenomena. I have gathered descriptions of all types of supernatural creatures and beings from little people to giants, lycanthropes to poltergeists, demons to angels and just strange acting folks. I've looked at both sides of the supernatural, the serious side and the seldom seen whimsical side. However, the whimsical side is basically found in literature, both classical and contemporary. I truly enjoy conversing about the strange and ghostly adventures offered on the pages of literature. I really could go on for a long while talking about pieces of literature devoted to the subject of the supernatural.

I also make this statement in regard to the serious side of the supernatural. To me, the realm of the supernatural is very real, very serious, very deadly. I respect it very much. I do believe in all sincerety what is written in the Holy Scriptures in Ephesians 6:12 which states, "For we wrestle not against flesh and blood, but against principalities, against powers, against the rulers of the darkness of this world, against spiritual wickedness in high places."

The reason I have written this manuscript is simply for the purpose of writing it. I am a Seneca Indian; I reside on the Allegany Indian Reservation in New York State. I want to say this: usually when an Indian pens any item there seems to be an automatic feeling that he or she is

attempting to make a cultural statement, a racial statement or a statement to preserve a certain item. I am not
making any such claim. I simply want to share some
tales of the supernatural with whoever will read them.
However, I do feel there is a uniqueness in the fact that
the stories compiled in this brief collection are entirely
Indian, told by Indians to Indians. They are not cultural;
they are not sacred; they are simply stories. My desire to
share these stories stems from their uniqueness. I write
solely from my feelings and experiences.

Growing up on an Indian reservation is a unique experience. Naturally there were differences in my upbringing from the upbringing of any non-Indian. One of the
things we had, was time with the old folks. The old folks
always had time to tell us things, and on hot or chilly
nights, they told us ghost stories. This was a very valuable thing—time with the old folks. My children will
never know this valuable experience, what is was or what
it meant. Hopefully, through this manuscript, I can
share just a touch of this time for them.

I remember these nights very well. In my situation I
remember warm moonlit nights. Haze covered the fields
and always hung like a grey ribbon above the river. Fire-
flies always added a personal meaning. On such nights,
we would come to them and say, "Ma," (we usually called
our grandmother "Ma") "tell us some ghost stories." We
gathered on the rough plank porch and she would spin a
tale to stand our hair on end. We delighted in terror. Our
days went on and, finally, the days became our children's. In the march of days we lost the old folks, a treasure lost. Some of our children got to know their great-
grandparents, but the time together on a moonlight
summer night is gone. The children today get a share of
spooky stories, but the stories come in the form of reruns
of "The Outer Limits" or "The Twilight Zone" or a Disney
fantasy.

The stories I have written are composites. Over the
years, I have heard many stories which were basically
the same. Each storyteller told it a little bit differently.
Some differences were minor while others were vastly
different in detail. The major difference came with how
much detail the storyteller wished to tell or not to tell,

but the storyline was basic. In this manuscript, I have taken different items from each basic story and condensed them into one basic story. Two or three of these stories are basically verbatim. After a number of these stories, I have added a personal comment.

In attempt to create a feeling, I have employed the colloquial language of my people, circa 1949–1952. This is how I heard the stories. I hope it is authentic.

I wish for the reader to imagine a Seneca storyteller. He is a hard-working man with signs of advancing age on his face. He can still work the woodpile with the best of them. Usually, he wears a red plaid flannel shirt with suspenders crossing down to his waistband. He has on heavy workshoes. It is eveningtime, and try to picture the time as being early autumn. Grandmother is busy shaving splints and grandfather sets himself down by the woodstove and adjusts the kerosene lamp. He waits for us and we come to him and say, "Grampa, tell us ghost stories." He would blow out a big puff of smoke and he would begin, "... Now this happened one time ... ."

The Lights

Now I'm going to tell you about the lights. There are lots of people who have seen these lights at one time or another. You always see them at night. They're little round lights and they are usually yellow or blue and sometimes orange. You see them everywhere; sometimes down by the river; across the river on the tracks; in the woods; around somebody's house or even up in the trees. Lots of times you see them at night when you go out to the baghouse or when you go out to get wood at night. They're all over the place. Whenever the old folks saw these lights they would always say, "... look, there goes a witch ..." or "... there's somebody watching you ..." Some of the people acted like they got scared but I think they did this just to scare the kids. Because the lights never hurt anybody. Except for one man I know of.

Now this guy wasn't afraid of the lights because he saw them everywhere because he was always going somewhere. He was always doing something. Hunting, fishing, spotting, going up town, cutting paper wood and things like that. He used to live in a shack by himself. He used to have only canvas to cover his windows. On hot nights he would leave all the windows uncovered and just lay around. Lots of times there was some one there visiting with him and they usually stayed until early morning. They used to talk about anything and listen to the radio. They used to tell a lot of ghost stories to each other. On nights when there was nobody there to visit him, this guy would just lay there listening to the radio and just look out the windows. During these times he could see the lights way off at the other end of the field. He used to tell people that he wasn't afraid of the lights because he was used to them.

One night he came home late from town. It was a hot night so he didn't bother to cover his windows. Since he was tired out, he went right to sleep. After a while he woke up. He said that he felt like somebody was watching him. So he turned over to see who it was. He thought that he saw a light just as he opened his eyes but it disappeared that fast. It didn't scare him and he just went right back to sleep. But the next night the same thing happened. So he thought about it and he decided to stay up the next night to see if it would happen again. So the next night he stayed awake. Just after midnight he saw a light come from over the hill which was across the river. But when it got down in the valley it went out of sight. So he waited for a long time and nothing happened. So he began to get tired of waiting and decided to go to bed. Just as he was about to go to sleep, he saw a blue light come over the roof of a house which was close by. It was moving real slow and it turned and began to come straight for his shack. Just as it got to the door, it disappeared. So he sat up and decided to wait for a while to see what would happen next. He stayed awake for a long time and it was nearly light when he decided to go back to bed again. This time he went right to sleep. He didn't know how long he had been sleeping, but all of a sudden he was awakened by a real sharp pain at the bottom of his spinebone. He said that it felt like somebody had stuck a real long needle in his back. He jumped right up and he saw a blue light fly away from him and it stopped by the door for a second. Then it took off real fast, back over the house again, across the river and back up and over the hill from which it came. It flew so fast that it took only a second to go back over the hill which was about a mile away. The light never came back to bother this guy again. Even though this light bit him, this guy still isn't scared of them. But he says that he thinks the light bit him because he was always saying the lights didn't scare him. He thinks that the lights only wanted to get some respect from him.

(It was not so long ago when this story was related to me. The subject of lights is a stable item in the realm of the supernatural. Every area of every country has its version of light stories. In regard to my own situation; there has been an advent of so-called "modern living" among my people. Indeed, it was almost instantaneous. However, with this advent, the lights have come with us; for I have personally seen these lights out and about our "modern" settlements. In treetops, rooftops and at windows. When discovered, the lights speed away at a truly fantastic rate of speed and disappear into the darkness. It is a real thrilling experience to watch one do so. The lights have been with us since the beginning of time and they will be with us until the end of time.)

The Car Wreck

One time there was a bad car wreck and three men were killed. It was a real bad one.

Sometime later there was a carload of men coming back from drinking in the next town. The only guy awake was the driver because all the others were asleep or passed out. Then one of the tires went flat and he had to stop. He stopped in the very same place where the car wreck had happened. The driver got out to look at the flat tire and then he tried to wake up the others so they could help change the tire. But nobody wanted to get out or they just turned over and went back to sleep. The driver got mad at them but he knew that they wouldn't get out. So he started to change the tire by himself. Because he was drunk it took him a long time to get the car jacked up. He didn't have the jack set right either. Just as he got the wheel off the car, the jack slipped and the car crashed down on the ground. The bumper was laying on the ground and the jack couldn't be replaced under the bumper. By now the guy was really mad and he tried to wake up somebody again but they just kept snoring away. He tried once more to get the jack back under the car but he couldn't. So he just gave up and leaned against the car and took a big drink from his jug. Just then somebody walked up and stood in front of the car. This person asked if he could help out. The driver answered that he wanted help. The person said that he had two more friends with him and that they would help out if they could have something to drink. The driver said that he had enough for everybody. But the driver began to feel funny because he couldn't see the faces of these men who were going to help him. The headlights were shining toward the ground and he could only see their legs. Their shoes looked all dried up and cracked. The three men grabbed the car by the bumper and picked it up off the ground. They held it up until the driver was able to put the spare on. Then they let it back down. The driver turned around to say something to them but they had moved to the other side of the car out of the light. He asked if they wanted a drink now and they said that they did. So he opened the door to get out another jug. When he opened the door the inside light came on and he turned around to give them the jug. When he saw them in the light, he lost his breath and fell to the ground. He could not moved because he was so scared by what he saw.

All three men were dead men. They all had skull heads and they were destroyed. One had the top of his head scraped away. They moved forward and the man tried to scream. They took the jug and each one took a good long drink. They put the jug down and they moved away back into the darkness. The man on the ground tried to yell and tried to get up but he couldn't. Just then his brother looked out the window and saw him laying on the ground. He got out of the car and went over to help his brother off the ground. The driver told his brother what just happened. Then they went and woke up the rest of the men in the car. They told them what just happened too. They all got scared. So they poured out some whiskey onto the ground and said some words to the ghosts which were just there. Then they all got back into the car and left there in a hurry.

The Blind Man and the Deaf Man

Now this happened one time. There were two men who lived together. One was blind but he could hear real good. The other man was deaf but he had good eyesight. They lived together so that they could help each other get along. They raised pigs, chickens and goats. They had a garden, too. They used to sell some of the vegetables, eggs and goat's milk. The people never made fun of these men because everybody liked and respected them for the way they got along. These men did the best they could. They hardly ever went anywhere except to town now and then. Since they never went anywhere, they usually went to bed early.

One night there was some noise from the area where the animals were kept. The guy who could hear woke up the other man and told him to go and see what was going on. He went downstairs and looked out and saw a great big dog around the animal pens. So he threw something at it and scared it away. He told his friend what he saw and said that he didn't think the dog was from the neighborhood. It might have come from across the river or maybe somebody from town had dumped it off.

A few nights later the same dog came back and did the same thing. And it came back the next night too. But this time the men decided to shoot the dog if it came back again. So the next night they were waiting. Just after midnight the dog came sneaking around the animal pens. The blind man heard the dog coming so the other man was ready when the dog came into sight. He fired and the dog fell down and started to scream and roll around. The man who could hear became frightened because the screams sounded more human than dog. Just then the dog jumped up and ran screaming into the woods. By now some of the neighbors who heard the strange screaming came running over to see what was going on. The two men told them what happened. They decided to go right after the dog. They got their flashlights and guns and went into the woods after the dog. In the woods they could follow the blood. They could tell it was a big dog by the size of the deep prints. They followed the prints to the river and then they turned back toward the road. They noticed that the prints were becoming different. A little further on they all saw something which scared everyone. The dog tracks had turned into human footprints. Right away the men knew what had come in the night to bother the two men. The trackers followed the blood and tracks to a house. They didn't go in or get too close to it. But they could see the blood clots lead across the lawn.

The people didn't see the man who lived in that house for a while. A short time later the people found out that this man had suffered a bad gunshot wound.

Talking to Animals

This is a story of a man everybody talked about. They said that he was funny because he was always talking to animals. People would see him talking to dogs, cats, horses, goats and even chickens. He used to have two or three dogs around him all the time. He really liked cats a lot too. He was good to the animals as long as they behaved. He used to hit them with a stick if they were bad or they peed in the house or something. But as long as they behaved he treated each one good and they got to stay in the house. Sometimes when people went to his house they would see him talking to the dogs. Some of the people didn't like to see this and some even called him a witch. Most of the people used to say that he wasn't all there. But they didn't say anything when they would ask him to do work for them. He used to do jobs like splitting wood, digging or weeding. Sometimes he would pound splints or sharpen axes. Then he didn't even charge them much either. Maybe just a quarter or fifty cents. But when he came into the house to get paid, they would watch every move he made because they thought he would steal something. But he never did. One time he was wiring a stovepipe and the lady who owned the house kept peeking out at him. She watched him as he began to climb down the ladder and saw him find a bat under the roof eave. He reached out and picked up the bat. He looked at it for a minute and then he put it to his ear. It looked as if he was listening to the bat. He put the bat back where he found it and he came down. The next day he didn't come back to finish the lady's roof. Nobody saw him for two days. When he came back to finish the job he was wearing new work clothes and shoes. Somebody made a joke that the bat told him where to find some money.

One day this very man told me this story himself. He said that he was standing behind his father's house one night and the house cat came up to him and began to purr and mew real loud. Right away he knew that the cat wanted him to follow him somewhere. So he followed the cat down the hill and into the woods. Every now and then the cat would stop and wait for him to catch up and move on again. Finally they came to a bank and down onto a plowed field. So he sat down on the bank and waited. The cat began to cry out and in a few minutes another cat answered in the distance. The cat called a few more times and in a few minutes another cat came across the field. It was a female. Then the man knew that the cat wanted him to meet his mate. So he knew that his father's house cat wanted him to meet his mate and it was like the two cats wanted his approval. So he began to pet them and say nice things to them. He said that they were purring real loud and that he liked the sounds that they were making. When he left them he said that he had a real good feeling inside of himself.

Later on that same summer this happened. I don't know who got this story but this is how it goes. One day one of his dogs came up to him and began to make noises. The man knew the dog wanted him to follow him so he did. The dog took him to a culvert just a little ways up the road. Inside the culvert the man found a big fold of money. There were all kinds of dollar bills in it. So he took the money and kept it with him at his house. He watched the culvert all summer but nobody ever came back to look in it. In the fall he used the money to buy a used car. He packed his things in it and loaded up the cats and dogs and just moved to the other reservation. He still lives there today and has a small family. He is still nice to everybody but now the dogs are not friendly at all. They are real fierce now. People don't like to go to his house at night because of the dogs. They act just like they are guarding something.

The Peeker

Now I'm going to tell you about a man who used to look into people's windows at night. Sometimes he used to stand on the road and look from there. Other times he would stand near the windows if there weren't any dogs to bark at him. One night a man caught him looking in his window. He chased the peeker around with a stick and hit him a couple of times and yelled at him to never look in the windows again. The next day this man told the peeker's grandma. She really got after the peeker and told him never to do this again. She told him if he didn't stop doing this, he would see something that he didn't want to see. So he told his grandma that he would stop looking into windows. But he didn't really mean it.

Then one day he didn't show up for work. He didn't go to work the next day either. So another man who worked on the same job with him went to see if he was sick. When he got there he found the peeker sick in bed with a bad fever. The peeker told him this story. He said that he had been out hunting a couple of nights ago. He said that he had to take a path which passed by an old lady's house. He said that he just happened to look into the lady's window as he passed by. She was making something and she just happened to look up when he looked in. She got real mad and began to yell at him, telling him to get out of there. Just as he turned to go he saw the old lady turn into a big grey cat. The cat came out of the house and it was hissing and spitting. He got scared and he began to run down the path. Then he felt a real sharp pain on the back of his leg. He tried to run but the cat kept clawing up his legs. He fell down and the cat bit him on the face. He got up fast and turned around and kicked the cat into the weeds. Then he was able to get away from the cat. But the cat came out of the weeds and began to chase him again. The hair on the cat's back was standing straight up. The man almost began to cry because he was so scared. Then the cat caught him again and really took a deep bite into his leg and then let go and ran back the other way. The man could hardly run any more because the cat bite hurt so much. His pant legs were all ripped up and bloody.

The peeker showed the other man his legs. They were covered with deep cuts and scratches and they were a bad color and all swollen up. A day later he had to go to the hospital because he was getting worse. He nearly lost a leg but he finally got better. He never looked into windows after that.

One More Story

I will tell one more story. An old lady told me this one
when I was a young boy. It was about her.

Now this happened one time. When she was a young
girl she used to live with different families because she
was an orphan. She would stay with one family for a
while and then move with another one for a while. She
was well liked and she worked hard to support her keep.
She liked to stay with old folks because she liked to help
them more. She was willing to do the heavier work for
them. She worked hard all the time.

One time she was staying with some old people who
lived a little ways back in the woods. It was cool on this
night so the man made a fire in the woodstove. It was
just beginning to turn into cold nights. Fall was just
beginning. The ladies were busy shelling beans and the
man was making basket handles. Just then there was a
bumping sound at the window in the bedroom. So the
man got up, took a lamp and went to see what was hap-

pening. When he looked he saw a pig looking in at him and it was bumping its nose against the window. It looked like it was trying to break the window. He yelled at it and it got down and ran off. He grabbed his stick and went outside to look around. When he came back in he said that the tracks went behind a tree and disappeared. Then the old man told the orphan girl to wait in the other room while he and the old woman went into the bedroom to check something. When they came back out they told the girl that she had to stay with a neighbor tomorrow night.

When the next evening came she was ready to go away for the night. The old folks told her that they would see her in the morning. So she left and went to the neighbors. She was almost there when she stuck her hand in her pocket and found the old man's snuff can. She knew that he would want it so she turned right around and started to take it back. She took her time because she figured that there was no rush. In a little while she could see the lights of the house so she stopped for a minute to take a short break. When she was standing there she saw something move into the light. It was the big pig again and it was going right back to the same window. She bent down to pick up a big stone to throw at the pig. Just as she started to go toward the pig, a light came from the back door and two big black cats came moving out of the house and went in opposite directions around the house. All of a sudden the pig began to squeal and she could hear the cats really hissing and spitting. She could see the pig stomping away with one of the cats clawed to its back. Then she saw a man come out of the brush and sneak into the open back door. She never saw this man before but she could see that he was carrying a big stick. So she ran to the house to protect the old folks. Just as she got to the door the man was coming out. She saw that he was stealing something, so she threw the stone and hit him on the face. He stumbled backwards and dropped two tin cans that he was carrying. She bent down to pick up a chunk of wood to use as a club but the man clubbed her with his stick and knocked her down. But she was tough and she got right back up. She clubbed the man across the back while he was trying to pick up the two tin cans. He fell down and dropped his stick. She rushed and picked it up first and clubbed him with it. She noticed that the stick had some kind of metal on the tip. When she hit the man again, he cried out in a real strange voice. Just then the two black cats came running around the house. They attacked the man and began to bite and claw at him. He tried to kick them but they were too fast for him. He ran off into the woods and the cats chased right after him. The girl could hear them fighting off in the woods. Then she threw the stick down and went inside to look for the old couple. They were not there. She went outside to call for them but they didn't answer. She saw the two tin cans laying on the ground, so she reached down to pick them up. But when she did, she got a real bad burn on her hand and fingers because the cans were real hot. It made her cry out. She got a rag and wrapped it around the cans and took them back inside and put them on the table. Then she sat down to wait for the old folks, and she wrapped a cold towel around her hand. In a few minutes the two black cats came into the house and they stopped and saw the girl sitting there. Then they turned and went back outside. The girl wanted to watch the property so she stayed there for the rest of the night. But she was afraid the pig or the man might return again.

In the morning the old folks came in. They said that they had spent the night with neighbors who lived way up the road. They said that they were all tired out from the long walk home. The girl didn't quite understand them because she knew that they could both walk for a long ways because they were used to walking. The girl told them what happened and they said that they were glad that she stayed and watched the place for them. Then the old lady took the two cans and put them back in the bedroom. Then they told the girl not to ever tell anyone about what happened. The girl promised never to tell.

About two months later the old folks asked the girl to watch the house because they had to go away for the night. So she did. The next day the old folks returned and told her that they had fixed it so that she would get the house when they passed away. This made the girl cry and she hugged both of them. They told her that they did this because she had given them extra time to live. The next day the girl saw the old lady put the two tin cans in a basket and take them somewhere.

In the springtime when the snow was just about all gone, some hunter found a frozen body of a man in the woods. Nobody knew who he was but they could tell that he was killed by a wildcat. There were claw marks and bites all over his head and neck. The papers in his pocket were too wet to read but one address could just about be made out and all that said was North Carolina.

About five years later the girl inherited the house. Then a short time after that she married a good man and they moved to town. The old folks had also left some money for her. The man got a good job on the railroad and he finally retired from there. They had three kids and these people lived to a good old age.

When I was young the story of the girl and the black cats got out and I heard it a couple of times. It was scary because I knew where the house was then. I got to know this girl when she was older and I liked her. Sometimes when we kids used to ask her, she would show us the burn scars on her hand and fingers.

That's enough stories for now.

Jane A. Kresovich

Beth Brant

I was born May 6, 1941. I'm a Bay of Quinte Mohawk, a mother, a grandmother, a foster parent. I started writing at the age of forty and it has been a difficult process for me. Economic realities, Indian invisibility, the lack of "formal, Euroamerican education", have taken their toll—yet at the same time these things have made me the kind of writer I am. I like to think I am continuing the long journey of being a storyteller that my people first began. And I want to tell the stories that nobody wants to hear—stories of working-class lives, gay lives, Indian lives—stories that refuse to fit an image of romance and sentimentality. I live in Detroit.

Indian Giver

ONE

Grandpa had chickens. In our backyard in urban Detroit, he had built a coop with little nests, but the chickens ran wild.

He gave them names. Mohawk names. His favorite was Atyo, which means *brother-in-law*. Said that the chicken's eyes had a look in them that reminded him of one of his relatives. It was useless to tell Grandpa that chickens were female and should have female names. He said it didn't matter, now we would have plenty of eggs and poultry to eat. But when it came time to kill the first hen, Grandpa couldn't do it. Said it was like killing one of the family. And didn't Atyo look at him with those eyes, just like brother-in-law, and beg not to have its head chopped off? The hens multiplied.

We had lots of eggs to eat. Grandma and Grandpa even boxed them up and sold them to the neighbors. Grandpa was happy with this arrangement. The rest of us. . . . Well, we had to step lightly in the yard, and Grandma mumbled about hanging clothes on the line and stepping on chicken shit and my, it made a mess of her shoes.

Some of the hens died of natural causes. Some died from Kitty, the twelve-year-old tomcat that bore no resemblance to his name and probably never had. But if we found a dead hen, Grandma and Mama plucked the feathers and made a stew. Pretty tough the meat was, but Grandpa would say, "See this was a good idea of mine; no sense in killing happy chickens. Let them die of their own accord."

We laughed as we chewed and chewed and chewed the tough meat. And ate eggs on the side, of course.

TWO

Each Christmas, Grandma had this plan that we'd have a bigger tree than the year before. The front room was pretty small, but she'd have measured the tree from the previous year, wrote down the measurements in her notebook, and then set out to find the perfect tree for this year. Sometimes it was embarrassing to have Grandma get out her tape measure and measure the trees in the lot down the street. A bunch of us kids had to go with her, each year our number increasing in order to carry the heavy balsam back to our house.

One year we couldn't get the tree through the door. Grandpa came out with a saw.

"Joseph Marcus, what in heaven's name are you going to do?"

"Margaret, there's only one way to get this tree in the house, and that's by cutting off the branches and gluing them back on once we get the tree in the front room."

"You're crazy," Grandma protested. But then, she gave in to the suggestion.

After all the big branches were cut off, we managed to get the tree in the front room where its trunk proved to be too big for the treestand.

Grandma said, "Now what, big smart man?"

He ran to the fruit cellar, coming up with a tin bucket. He got my dad to mix some cement, placed the tree in the bucket, then poured the cement inside. Grandpa said he'd just stand there holding the tree, waiting for the cement to harden. He stood for a long time.

Grandma went into the kitchen to help my mom make the bread for the week. I could hear them in the kitchen, laughing. Grandma and Mom made trips to the front room, Grandma saying, "Still there, smart man?"

"Still here, smart woman."

In the meantime, us kids were collecting sawed-off branches and bringing them in, wondering how Grandpa was going to fix this one. One of us even asked, "Hey Grandpa, how are we going to get these branches back on the tree? It don't seem likely." But Grandpa had faith. He'd find the right branches, they would fit perfectly, and the glue would magically stick.

It didn't work out that way. One thing was that somehow he hadn't held the tree straight, and it leaned to one side. But Grandpa said the leaning side could go towards the window and no one would ever know. Billy, one of the littler kids, said, "Grandpa, it still looks like it's leanin', like it's going to crash through the window."

This time Grandpa didn't answer.

The glue wouldn't stick. Even with all of us holding the branches tight against the trunk, they just fell off.

By now, Grandma was getting mad. But Grandpa retaliated by saying if she didn't have such notions about bigger trees every year, none of this would have happened.

There was truth to this claim, but as Grandma said, "Well, I admit I get notions, but it's too late to talk about that. You, Joseph Marcus, *you* take the cake!"

That Christmas we had this funny tree. But it was even funnier on Christmas morning. Grandma had bought little dolls for all the girls, dolls dressed in their national costumes. It had been her idea to decorate the tree with these dolls perching on branches. Since there were no branches to perch on, Grandpa hated to waste the glue, so he put a drop on each doll's foot and arranged them at intervals around the skinny tree.

On Christmas morning when we came downstairs the dolls looked sort of crazy. Most of them were hanging upside down, skirts over their heads, only their white underpants showing. Trying to get them off the tree was another matter. The kitchen knife was brought forth and each doll sawed off the tree. I had a Spanish doll with a black lace mantilla and a sliver of balsam underneath her feet.

We laughed a lot over that tree, Grandpa saying, "See, I knew it would work out."

The next year, Grandpa nailed the Christmas tree to the floor. But that's another story.

Daddy

"One time I remember," Daddy says.

"The time every day I went out and looked for work. You know, day labor. Everybody standin' in lines, beggin'. We woulda done just about anythin'. Them days, the thirties, we begged!

I heard they was hirin' men at the salt mines, loadin' salt onto the railroad cars. I got there at the right time, cause no sooner had I signed my name on the paper, I was called into the yard. I was lucky that day.

Some men, they was usually white, they got to mine the salt. Go underneath and dig it up. That paid the best. But I was happy with the work. Got hired on for the day. Eight hours. Hard work.

I couldn't talk American. Talked Canadian, eh? They asked me why I talked funny. I says, 'I'm Indian.' So they say, 'Well Chief, get to work.'

Now that mornin' I'd given blood for a friend of mine, laid up in hospital. We had the same type. Indian.

The white woman who took the blood, she said I should relax and take it easy. But those days, you couldn't afford to relax. It was every minute you thought about a job, about feedin' your family. It's the same now. People think about workin', not relaxin'.

Well, I got to workin', throwin' the bags of salt in the box cars. They were heavy. Maybe fifty or a hundred pounds.

We stood in a line, five of us. The line went up, endin' with me on the ladder in front of the box cars. Yes, the salt ended with me. I was the last and threw it in the car. My arms were numb, eh?

Sometimes the bags broke, and the salt came spillin' out on us. The boss yelled and yelled, makin' us sweep it up and put it back in the bags. Some of us, we laughed at him.

I remember, his face was so red, and he worried more

about salt than he did about us. But see, that was his job, eh?

That's the way it was in those days. And it's still like that. I never knew anybody a union didn't help.

That day I had a sandwich your ma had made for me. Pork, I think it was. On fry bread. It was in my pocket, wrapped in wax paper, but it made a stain on my pants.

You know how you can remember funny things about the past? Well, that day, I remember the boss's red face and that stain on my pants. And the man I shared my sandwich with.

He was a white man, and he was real hungry. Told me he had a big family, nine or ten kids, I think. Yes, that's what it was.

Well, I ate my part of the sandwich and was gettin' dizzy all the while. I guess the blood-givin' made me a little weak. I don't know if I can make it for the whole eight hours, but I eat some more and sit for a few.

Then the boss asks do I want to work an extra four hours. I say yes! Not thinkin', but still I'm thinkin' about your mom, your sister, your grandma and grandpa. It makes sense to say yes to work.

So I work, eh?

The dizziness went away. I think I scared it.

I got home around eleven o'clock that night. Your mom, she fixes me a bowl of soup and some tea. I go to bed and sleep for twenty-four hours. Straight.

Your mom, she tries to get me up the next day. I can't move. I slept for twenty-four hours!

And the worst part is that I missed goin' out to look for work the next day. Your ma, she was mad, but then she wasn't.

I figure I worked twelve hours in two days and missed out on four more hours work. That made *me* mad.

I never gave blood to an Indian again."

for all my Grandmothers

A hairnet covered her head.
a net
encasing the silver strands.
A cage confining the wildness.
No thread escaped.

(once, your hair coursed down your back
streaming behind
as you ran through the woods.
Catching on branches,
the crackling filaments
gathered leaves.
Burrs attached themselves.
A redbird plucked a shiny thread
for her nest,
shed a feather that glided
into the black cloud and
became a part of you.
You sang as you ran.
Your moccasins
skimmed the earth.
Heh ho oh heh heh)

Prematurely taken
from the woodland.
Giving birth
to children that grew
in a world that is white.
Prematurely
you put your hair up and
covered it
with a net.

Prematurely grey
they called it.

Hair Binding.

Damming the flow.

With no words, quietly
the hair fell out
formed webs on your dresser
on your pillow
in your brush.
These tangled strands
pushed to the back of a drawer
wait for me.
To untangled
To comb through
To weave together the split fibers
and make a material
Strong enough
to encompass our lives.

Pam Colorado

"Skanagoah", greeting you in Oneida, I ask, "the great Peace, are you in it?" From childhood to these adult years, the tree has guided, shaped and given direction to my life. But only recently have I become aware of the love, peace and kindness inherent in our woodland teachings.

Growing up in the Northwoods of Wisconsin the soft, furry moss layering these snags became my comforter. Deep, dark Tamarack, standing in its bed of needle covered earth permitted me to run silent through the forest — proper Indian style. And on fine, sunny days my cat and I lay on the warm split trunk of a pine, recently blown into Birch Lake. Pan fish liked the cool shadow of submerged branches and perhaps enjoyed the twin brace of brown and yellow eyes staring down at them.

Today these teachings sustain me as I nourish the next part of the tree — my three children. The tree teaches balance, cooperation, patience, trust and reaching out, in all relations, but especially in marriage. And I am married to a Haida named. . . . Woody.

Recent work has increasingly focused on Skanagoah, which is also our word for the tree. Teaching Social Welfare for the University of Calgary, my passion is Native Science, as taught to us by the tree! We, the tree and I, are happy to share our thoughts with you in the *New Voices from the Longhouse*. Nyaweh.

Oneida

moist night air
hangs heavy
over still
stalks of corn
  bathed
in light
of full moon
i move
silent
naked
through the fields
light my smoke
and dream of home

Raven Story

Around nine, Slakum cranked open the kitchen window of the aging trailer home and peered into solid black night. The ocean, only fifty feet away, was impossible to see. Rain needled her face. Suddenly the wind shifted; fingers of cold air darted through the open window, scooping and scattering the pile of freshly typed pages to the floor. Struggling to hold down what was left of the stack and at the same time close the window, Slakum muttered. "Damn the rain, damn these people, damn this isolation!"

For six days the tiny island village of Awah had been cut off from the world. Fog hanging in the passes meant no seaplanes and that meant no food in the store and worse, no mail!

"The mail", she chuckled dryly. Incredible how important it had become. Like some pigeon in a psych experiment, she imagined herself trekking back and forth to the post office. Day after day, back and forth on any pretext she'd heard a plane, like the pigeon pecking endlessly. At least she could talk with the postmistress. That is, until today. Walking through the door, gum boots wet and squeaking on the muddy floor, Slakum saw a hand printed sign, "NO MAIL YET TODAY". The postmistress sat in the back cozily drinking coffee.

Sighing again, Slakum finished picking up the scattered pages. Her mind wandered back to the first days of her marriage to Kadah. He was so gentle, strong and bright; the first lawyer in his tribe. Leaning against the kitchen counter she thought how new and clear her sight had seemed, how beautiful were the snow capped mountains and the Eagles of Alaska soaring against them. Everything had seemed so good at first. She was confident that the ways of her own western tribe would unite here with these strange ocean people. Shaking her head, she marveled at her naivete. Surely Kadah had noticed. He might have cautioned her.

"Scaga, Scaga" they had called her . . . witch doctor. Praying and purifying in the backyard Sweat Lodge, they had been mocked by the locals and heard the jeers at the "primitive practices" of the "outside Indians". Those taunting voices still rang in her ears. The drunks and Christians calling names escalated to such crowds that Kadah feared for their safety and came home early from work one day and took down the lodge. Now only the bare ground remained. The black hole that had been the fire pit stared like a sad eye up into the stormy night.

Now Slakum jumped. Rubbing her chilled arms, she prayed aloud, "The Fire! God don't let the fire be out". Kadah was virtually marooned on the mainland, and the kindling and wood supply was nearly used up. The few fragments that remained were soaking wet. The fire must not die!

Hurrying to the woodstove, Slakum dragged the flannel cuff of her shirt down over her hand, grabbed the hot iron handle and threw open the stove door. Plenty of coals left, she groaned with relief. Just then, a gust of wind burst down the stove pipe spewing a cloud of ash and dust out the door enveloping her. Coughing and sputtering, she slammed it . . . too late! Smoke alarm buzzed its wasp voice through the hall and into the room of the sleeping children. Seizing a big piece of cardboard, Slakum ran through the trailer opening doors and frantically waving at the smoke. "Please don't let the kids wake up," she implored.

For days Slakum waited for a chance to write. Seven years of course work and research now only weeks from deadline. If only it weren't for village chores — packing wood, hauling water, washing clothes by hand. All the things easy down south were impossible here. She put the cardboard down and listened. The alarm was silent, tiny snores were peaceful in the bedroom.

"Only one more chore and I can get back to my writing" she thought and jumped into her storm coat. Stepping outside, she ran through the rain to the wood pile. "Good, there is a big wet chunk left." It could smolder until morning. She wrestled the slimy cedar into her arms and turned to go back inside. She screamed! Someone stood only a few feet away!

Slakum croaked, "Who's there!" Crunching footsteps in the gravel brought the figure nearer. Oh, it was a child! Wet shoulders were slouched and small hands thrust deep in her pockets. The little girl came closer. Slakum saw she was trembling.

"Ama! What are you doing out in this weather?" Looking into the tear-filled eyes of the child, she knew. Her parents must be drinking again.

"The kids are sleeping, dear." Slakum fought her desire to send the child away. Quickly she added, "but you better come in and dry off". Ama nodded and led the way up the steps. Inside Slakum started jabbing the logs onto the fire angrily. Impatient, fretting over this delay in her work, she fumed. "Damn these people". Looking at the child, cold, wet, probably sad, she thought and felt ashamed and loving. She heard herself say. "Do you want some hot cocoa?"

"All right", the small voice chirped. There seemed to be a new, little tone of hope in it.

As the crackle of cedar fire filled the room in bright warmth, the cocoa came to a bubble. Slakum poured two cups and the two of them sat down on the couch. In a while the little girl began to talk.

> They're having Bible study group down at the Church nearly every night now, and Mrs. Pach is so nice to me and the rest of the ladies too . . .

Images of the stout missionary wife filled Slakum's mind and muffled Ama's voice which seemed far away. The last thing this child needed was those vipers on her case . . .

Adopted at birth, Ama had been given to a couple with drinking problems. When she was nearly four, the couple divorced. It was then that the doctors noticed the hazing of the girl's right eye. The cancer took the vision completely. And the surgery which saved her life left her with one glass eye. Recently the mother had remarried, this time to the biggest drunk in town. With no income for doctors, the child had to continue wearing an eye fitted for her more than two years earlier. The other day, Ama said, she'd turned to see what her teacher wanted and the eye fell out right in front of everyone. The village kids squealed with glee. They hated Ama, for her early years in the city, for her differences and her gentleness. They were on her like a pack of dogs at the slightest chance.

Today, Slakum had looked out the window when Ama turned to face her tormenters. Charging into a group of three, the little girl fought wildly. She lost the fight and had a big bruise on her face to show for it. But she had fought. "Maybe now", thought Slakum, "maybe now, they'll leave her alone". But she doubted it.

Just then, the child's voice pulled Slakum back.

Mrs. Pach says if I pray to Christ and go to Church we could get saved. My Mom and Dad could quit drinking and I wouldn't have to worry any more. Sometimes I'm so afraid for my Mom. She says, 'Ama, don't every leave me. I'll die if you go'. And I don't know what to do. I wish I could go live with my first Dad down in Portland. He wants me to live with him and he's good to me. But I'm afraid for my Mom. I tell her, "mom, get a divorce. You and Al could still be friends. I'll stay with you".

I'm afraid something is going to happen . . . I can't sleep at night. They're always fighting . . . I prayed like they told me, but . . . Tonight they're really fighting. Al pushed my Mom against the wall and said if he caught her again . . . And that's when I left the house. I walked up here, Beach Way and found this feather. See, it looks just like yours, so I thought I would come here.

Looking down at the white Eagle feather clutched in the child's hand, Slakum choked up.

"Ama, come here. Let me hug you," she said. Holding the girl in her arms, Slakum continued. "Ama, anytime things are bad at home come over here". She wiped Ama's tears. Pointing to the feather, she said,

This feather you found, it's really good, Ama.
Indian way, we know it is a gift from Creator.

It's a way of letting you know you are loved.
Most of us wait a long time for such a wonderful blessing.
You are so young, yet you have this. What can it mean?

The woman and child talked on. Slakum sensed that the child needed something more. Suddenly she remember the photographs that had arrived on the last mail plane.

"Ama, would you like to see the pictures I took of the rock carvings at Blue Mountain?"

The child nodded. Searching through the piles of books and papers, Slakum began to think . . . The petroglyphs. It was the only real work Slakum had found in the village. Looking for connections, she had finally found this ancient, holy site. Most local people had never heard of the rocks and fewer had ever seen them. That first trip, as her skiff neared the site, chills swept over Slakum's body. Without thinking she jumped from the boat, offered tobacco and feverishly started to chalk in and photograph. There were hundreds of designs. But there was barely time for two visits, when fall winds and storms made the trip over open ocean impossible. Now only the handful of photographs remained to show for the high hopes she had had on this discovery.

Shuffling through the photographs, a wave of shame swept over Slakum. "How dumb can I be?" she thought. The single most prominent feature of the carvings was, EYES! In her excitement, Slakum dropped a picture. Instantly Ama snatched it up. She looked at the photo for a long time, then asked, "What's this one?"

For the first time Slakum saw a new aspect of the carving. Photographed upside down, she had not recognized the design until now. It was Raven with the sun in his beak! "Anmean, ahmeah," she whispered excitedly, something is happening! Shaking with a sense of the presence of spirits, Slakum explained:

Ama . . . this One is sacred. There is a very old old story behind it. You see, at one time, the world was in blackness. The only things that broke the Quiet were waves pounding argillite shores and the whisper of cockles on the beach.

In this place, Raven created human beings and the loneliness was ended. But People were like shadows moving in the darkness . . . they were afraid and unhappy.

Raven saw this and wondered how to help the people. But Raven is a trickster so naturally he thought of a plan to get light away from the man who had it.

Changing himself into a nettle floating in the stream, He was swallowed by the Man's daughter, when she came to drink. Later, she gave birth to a beautiful boy, who was really Raven. The man, who was no Raven's Grandfather, came to love the boy very much and really spoiled him.

So when Raven began fussing for the box that the sun was in, the Grandfather finally relented and let the boy play with it.

Slowly Raven child slid the lid from the box. LIGHT, wondrous Light radiated out, penetrating the darkness.

Quickly, the boy changed back into Raven. He seized the orb of Light in his beak and Flew to the smoke-hole. But the opening was narrow; he got stuck for a few moments, and that's how Raven who was white to begin with, turned Black . . . from the soot and smoke.

When Raven broke free from the smoke-hole, he flew with the Light to the beach. Taking the disc, he broke it on a rock and threw the pieces to the sky. They became stars, Moon and Sun.

And that's what this rock picture is about. Raven has two different Eyes on this carving because he Sees two different ways. One is the regular way and the other is the Spirit way. Raven is a Spirit Being.

Ama jumped up from the couch. "And me, what about me? I have two different Eyes! Do you think I could see like that some time?"

Fighting tears, Slakum answered.

"Child, there is no doubt. There hasn't been a traditional healer here in a long time. Maybe through you, the People will See Good again . . ."

The child interrupted.

"Can I use your phone to call my Dad in Portland? I've been trying for three days but couldn't get an answer at his house. I'll call collect."

Slakum nodded assent. As Ama began to dial, Slakum picked up the cocoa cups and walked back into the kitchen. Washing up the dishes, she could hear Ama say:

"Dad? Dad? I'm so glad I got you . . . I tried for three days . . . Dad, do you know what my Eyes mean? They mean I might be a Medicine person some day!"

Hearing the joy in the child's voice, Slakum's heart filled with pride. She mentally patted herself on the back for finding the exact right solution to the child's problems. But just as she began to enjoy her glory, she heard Ama say:

"How do I know? Dad, this OLD woman told me."

Hands suspended in sudsy water, Slakum heard a strange sound . . . her own laughter! OLD WOMAN?! Here she was, at 37, filled with triumph and pride – and this little girl had burst her bubble fast! Slakum laughed till her shoulders shook. Tears ran down her face . . . "Raven, you got me good this time!" she chuckled.

Hearing the receiver click down into the phone, Slakum grinned, composed herself and rounded the corner into the living room. "Well," she asked, "What did your Dad have to say?"

Ama answered: "Well, I told him about the Raven rock and the Eyes and how I might be a spiritual person."

"What did your Dad say?" Slakum queried.

"He said, 'You know I believe it.' " Ama pulled on her jacket.

"Where are you going, Ama?"

"I'm going home. They'll be asleep now". Ama grabbed her feather and the two stepped out into a still night. The rain and wind were gone. Bright stars glittered in an inky sky.

As Ama walked away, Slakum handed the photo to her. "Keep it; it belongs with you."

Slakum waited and listened to the small feet slapping the wet earth of the road. When she heard Ama's front door slam, Slakum climbed back up to the trailer. Standing on the top step, thinking about the night and her unexpected promotion to "Elder", she thought she heard the words of Nana, Kadah's 100 year-old Grandmother:

And the Way the Old People used to tell it
He was a wonderful Bird!

"And I believe it" she said to herself and the cold listening, night air.

NOTE: *A special thanks to Mary Tall Mountain for her editing and to Viola Morrison, Haida Elder for her help.*

Americanization

spirit
cries
of freedom
waters
wind
and pine

choked in
Twinkies
Bandstand
Buses
caught
in
leaden skies

Indian Science

"... This is what Raven did for us ... The shelter is the tree ... "

Indian science, often understood through the tree, is holistic. Through spiritual processes, it synthesizes or gathers information from the mental, physical, social and cultural/historical realms. Like a tree the roots of Native science go deep into the history, body and blood of the land. The tree collects, stores and exchanges energy. It breathes with the winds, which tumble and churn through greenery exquisitely fashioned to purify, codify and imprint life in successive concentric rings — the generations. Why and how the tree does this is a mystery but the Indian observes the tree to emulate, complement and understand his/her relationship to this beautiful, life-enhancing process.

The Meaning of Science

To the Indian, the tree is the first spirit or person on Earth. Indeed, the tree which oxygenated Earth's atmosphere, is the precursor to our human existence. Because of its antiquity it is a respected Elder, but the greatest power of Native science lies in the reasons behind the tree's existence.

When discussing the origins of the tree Chief Donawaak, Tlingit Elder, says:

This is where stories begin; there is no story before this . . . When Raven spirit and Black Raven are working on this land, they put coves in it where you can come in when it's blowing — a place where you can come ashore.

My Great Grandfather who told this story to me said — the cove is where you're going to be safe. If you pass that harbour you're not going to go very far . . . you will tip over or drown. But if you come to the cove you will be safe. This is what Raven did for us. The shelter is the tree.

You could get under the tree and stay there overnight. All this is what the Raven did . . .

From these words we see that Native science has a sacral basis and that its teachings are grounded in the natural world. The Navajo and the Natural World are one; he expresses that unity in this way:

The foundation, you have to know your roots, where you are coming from. It is understood that we all come from God, God created us. But you have to understand in your own Indian way where your roots are. You see a tree that is weak, about to give up. Sometimes you find people like that. Why is that tree just barely making it. Because the roots are not strong. If the roots are solid and strong, then you see the tree is strong and pretty. It can withstand cold, hot weather and winds. The human has to have those roots because we are growing too. The Great Spirit put us here with nature. We have to understand the nature. That is why we understand how an animal behaves. That is why we have to talk to them. We don't pray to them, we talk to them because they breathe the same air we do. We are put here with them. We are also a part of the plant life. We are always growing; we have to have strong roots.

Indeed all of life can be understood from the tree.

. . . just after the earth's crust was formed Raven (the Creator) made the tree. Why did he make this tree? He made it to shelter us. Even before Raven broke light on the World, people took shelter from the tree. And after he broke light, look what you're sitting on, what's above you, it comes from the tree.

And that's where the Tlingit gets his canoe, his house, his clothes – everything. The Raven put it there for him (the people).

And look, what's growing under that tree? The grass. In the spring the Bear comes down to eat that grass and the wolf, the moose and the mountain goat. All these things, they come. And the berries, growing there – salal, salmonberry, huckleberry and beneath them, the plants – the medicine. All that, it comes from the tree.

So the roots and their functions form the basis of Native scientific methodology. Seeking truth and coming to knowledge necessitates studying the cycles, relationships and connections between things. Indeed, a law of Native science requires that we look ahead seven generations when making decisions!

Principles of Native Science

Laws and standards govern Native science just as they do western science. In an Indian way, Bear who is the North represents knowledge, healing and comfort. The Bear is also fierce; his claims are non-negotiable. Western science understands Bear in terms of rigor, reliability, and validity.

In the spring Bear marks his territory on the tree. Stretching as far as possible, Bear uses his claws to score the tree. Other bears passing by are challenged to meet this standard. If they cannot reach the mark they leave the territory. For the Native scientist, the tree is not merely science but science interwoven inseparably with life. We meet the mark or die. Like the Bear passing through, no one watches us; the science relies on utmost integrity.

Native science assumes its character through power and peace. Vine Deloria, noted Lakota scholar, discusses its principles:

> Here power and place are dominant concepts — power being the living energy that inhabits and/or composes the universe, and place being the relationship of things to each other . . . put into a simple equation: Power and place produce personality. This equation simply means that the universe is alive, but it also contains within it the very important suggestion that the universe is personal and, therefore, must be approached in a personal manner . . . The personal nature of the universe demands that each and every entity in it seek and sustain personal relationships. Here, the Indian theory of relativity is much more comprehensive than the corresponding theory articulated by Einstein and his fellow scientists. The broader Indian

idea of relationship, in a universe very personal and particular, suggests that all relationships have a moral content. For that reason, Indian knowledge of the universe was never separated from other sacred knowledge about ultimate spiritual realities. The spiritual aspect of knowledge about the world taught the people that relationships must not be left incomplete. There are many stories about how the world came to be, and the common themes running through them are the completion of relationships and the determination of how this world should function.

Deloria notes that there is no single Native science; each tribe or Nation follows ways specific to a locale. However, the tree and the Bear are nearly universal. From South America to the Arctic, the tree and all that it implies has been guiding and shaping the thought of Native people since the dawn of humanity. Those who follow this natural science do so in search of balance, harmony or peace with all living relations. Iroquois call this SKANAGOAH.

THE GOAL OF INDIAN SCIENCE

Skanagoah, literally interpreted as "great peace", is the term used to describe the still, electrifying awareness one experiences in the deep woods. This feeling or state of balance is at the heart of the universe and is the spirit of Native science. For the western-educated audience, the notion of a tree with spirit is a difficult concept to grasp. The English language classifies reality into animate and inanimate objects, with most things falling into the inanimate classification. Native languages do not make the same distinction. As Deloria says, the universe is alive. Therefore, to see a Native speaking with a tree does not carry the message of mental instability; on the contrary, this is a scientist engaged in research!

Put another way, western thought may accede that all natural things are imbued with energy. Much like the electromotive force in a capacitor, the force of the energy is transmitted without there being a direct flow of energy. If you had a piece of wire, electricity would travel from one end to the other uninterrupted. But if you put a capacitor in the line, the force is transmitted from one side to the other without there being a direct flow of electricity from one side to the other. This is how energy is transferred from tree to tree and tree to person without there being a direct flow of energy. The spiritual energy of a tree isn't transmitted directly but rather its life force is felt. Like a capacitor, the thickness of the dielectric, the physical distance between the person and the tree is not important; the exchange still occurs.

This exchange suggests that human beings play a vital part in Skanagoah. Western thought teaches the value of the specialist, especially to the masses who are mostly generalists. In an Indian way, we may think of the Bear as a specialist; indeed, if I compete with the Bear in his own environment and on his terms, there is no way I can match his proficiency. But the generalist in this case, human beings, determine the continuance of Bear's habitat. We are related, we are all one, life and death, good and bad, we are all one. The Indian acknowledges this and so discovers the most liberating aspect of Native science: LIFE RENEWS and all things which support life are renewable.

Kahionhes

Katsi Cook

Katsi Cook is an early founder of *Akwesasne Notes*. In the 1970's she traveled extensively with The White Roots of Peace. She has been an active midwife since 1978. A lecturer on women's health practices, she is currently an organizer on women's health and toxicity issues with the Akwesasne Environment Project.

As a writer, she has been published in a number of magazines including *Mothering, Akwesasne Notes, Ms, Northeast Indian Quarterly* and *Daybreak*. Excerpts from her work are published in two books dealing with medical issues.

The Women's Dance:

Reclaiming Our Powers

Traditional Values

It is important to begin at the beginning. In everything the People do, they start at the beginning. When I asked, "How do we teach the young about birth?" I was told, "Begin with the story of the first birth." So, we turn to our origins to understand women's ways. The Creation stories, the cosmologies, contain the world view and values of Indigenous Peoples. They are the spiritual foundation of traditional communities, and an important place to start when we need to understand how to deal with the problems we face here and now today.

In Iroquois cosmology, a pregnant woman in the sky world wanted some bark from the roots of the Great Tree that stood at the center of the universe. In digging up the roots for her, her husband made a hole in the floor of the sky world, and the pregnant woman curiously peeked through the hole. As she bent and looked through the empty space and ocean far below, she fell. She grabbed at the edges of the hole, but she slipped through. In her hands were bits of things that grow in the sky-world. She landed on the back of a great turtle, and was aided by the animals to found a new firmament. As the woman walked in a circle around the clod of dirt supplied by a muskrat from the bottom of the ocean, the earth began to grow. She planted the things she carried in her hands from the sky-world. She continued to circle the earth, moving as the sun goes. Her time came and she delivered a daughter. They both continued to walk in a circle around the earth, and lived on the plants that were growing there. A man appeared; some say it was the West Wind. The daughter of Sky Woman was soon pregnant with twins, and these twins argued within their mother's body. They argued about their birth. The right-handed twin was born in the normal way, and the left-handed twin was born through his mother's armpit. This killed her. In the world outside their mother's body, they continued to quarrel. They buried their mother and from her grave grew corn, beans and squash, the "three sisters" which still sustain us, and Indian tobacco, which is used in ceremonies. The twins continued to quarrel and with their creative powers contested one another. From their contests they created the world, which was balanced and orderly.

In the way these things are told to us, these intricate stories which take many days to relate, there is room which motivates the individual to seek their own perception about life. This is why there are so many different versions of the Creation story. Different versions follow different threads of perception. And they all teach something about life, and the world. We learn about opposites, and a world that is neither all good nor all bad. We learn that the entire universe is a family, and we learn that the greatest good is harmony. We learn the responsibilities and original instructions that all Creation has in maintaining this harmony.

Moon Cycles, Earth Cycles

In the Native American consciousness, health is a matter of balance and harmony. Our old people maintained this balance by a sophisticated system of ceremonies and knowledge based on an awareness based on our relationship to everything in the universe and a respect for all life. Everything in Creation was expressed in dualities, such as male and female. Everything in Creation is paired and in balance with each other. The winds, the rains, rocks and rivers, all have their male and female. In between these two poles is the life force which comes to rest on Mother Earth.

A powerful force in our universe is the Sun. "Brothers and Sisters," Sitting Bull said, "the spring has come. The Earth has received the embraces of the Sun and we shall soon see the results of that love. Every seed is awakened and so has all animal life. It is through this mysterious power that we too have our being."

Some people say the energy from the Sun is too strong,

however, for the Earth to contain. Therefore, it reflects itself to the Moon. The Moon, the mother of the Universe, absorbs this excess energy. In this action she then reflects the Sun back to himself so that he will not overwhelm her, and she can make full use of his lifegiving power. The duality of male and female is basic in life. This concept finds its way even into the political systems of some Native communities, as with the Iroquois Confederacy where male and female sit in council together.

"I'll tell you, the women – they had the power. If you wanted to get anything done you had to go to your grandmother. If she agreed, you could take it to the clan mothers, and they would decide if they would take it to the Chiefs and put it through Council."

Ernie Mohawk, Seneca Elder

The Women's Community

In a traditional world, Native American women understood their bodies in terms of the Earth and the Moon. In the universal community of women, the Earth was perceived as our Mother from whom all Life comes. A Dene origin myth tells of the menstrual flow of the Earth by which vegetation and reproduction are possible. This flow, which we know as dew, was created from the maple dew of the horizontal skyblue and the female dew of darkness. Reproduction originated from this menstruation of the Earth. The Moon, our Grandmother, is the leader of all female life. She controls all things female or procreative. She causes movement of the great waters of reproduction, of birth itself, and the oceans. That the Grandmother Moon controls the forces of reproduction is basic to the health, or balance, of female life. The time of the menses is referred to as "my grandmother is visiting me."

The old women tell us, "A woman is like the Moon. When she is young and just becoming a woman, she is like the New Moon. She will usually menstruate on the New Moon. As she walks further into life, she reaches her peak and becomes like the full moon. She, too, is full and fertile. As she ages, she wanes with the Moon. Throughout life, as with every monthly cycle of fertility and purification, she wanes with the Moon. It is as if she were holding hands with her grandmother."

In *Kwakiutl Ethnography*, Franz Boaz says: "Pregnancy lasts ten moons after the last period. At the first appearance of the new Moon, in the last month of her pregnancy, she goes outside and prays to the moon for an easy delivery. This is done four times. The child is generally born at full moon of that month."

Grandma Moon's effect on the procreative waters was also known by the Wichita People: "The Spirit of the water, Woman Forever in the Water, is closely associated with the Moon Spirit, yet their functions differ: one creates life, the other makes possible its growth and continuation. As an illustration a woman desiring a child would not pray to the water spirit, but would address her supplication to the Spirit of the Moon, then when the child was born the mother implored the beneficence of the Water Spirit, the Moon Spirit, and included the Supreme Spirit." (Man Not Known On Earth. Curtis, Volume 19, *The North American Indian*).

Woman's Ways: Changing Women

In many Native American origin stories, puberty ceremonies were a gift to women from the Moon or other primal being. The ritual passage into womanhood was fundamental to the development and growth of a healthy woman. With much variation from nation to nation, this was generally a time of elaborate and joyful recognition of the appearance of the first menstrual flow which marked the change from girlhood to womanhood. "On the occasion of her first menses a Cahuilla girl was laid recumbent on a bed of brush and herbs heated in a trench. Covered with a blanket she remained there throughout three nights, while men and women danced and sang songs alluding to the institution of this custom by Moon and to the proper conduct of menstruating girls."

The puberty ceremony was perhaps the most important ceremony in the life of the Native American woman. At this time, she was isolated from the general community and, attended by her female relatives, was instructed in the skills and character essential for her survival in the community. There is a great wealth of anthropological and autobiographical information on Native women's experience at puberty.

Of the many remarkable stories told by and about Indian women concerning their passage into womanhood, all have common characteristics, although the ceremony itself was incidental to cultural variances. In *The Sacred*, Beck and Walters state that: "The patterns of behavior prescribed for menstruating women and pubescent girls were similar in their reasoning and objectives. Menstruation was equated with power which could be utilized for healing or curing. The power had to be recognized by a woman and others around her. When she adhered to the prescribed rules of behavior, this power was acknowledged."

Delfina Cuero, a Diegueno born in 1900, came of age in an area of California (San Diego) where the missionaries had done much to destroy traditional "pagan" ceremonies. In doing so, they also destroyed the moral, educational, and ethical systems by which the Diegueno lived their lives. "My grandmother told me about what they did to girls as they were about to become women. They had already stopped doing it when I became a woman.

"Grandmothers taught these things about life at the time of a girl's initiation ceremony. Nobody just talked about these things ever. It was all in the songs and myths that belonged to the ceremony. All that a girl needed to know to be a good wife, and how to have babies and to take care of them was learned at the ceremony, at the time when a girl became a woman. We were taught about food and herbs and how to make things by our mothers and grandmothers all the time. But only at the ceremony for girls was the proper time to teach the special things women had to know. Nobody just talked about those things, it was all in the songs. But I'm not old, they had already stopped having the ceremonies before I became a woman, so I didn't know these things until later. Some of the other girls had the same trouble I did after I was married. No one told me anything. I knew something was wrong with me but I didn't know what. One day I was a long way from home looking for greens.

I had terrible pain. I started walking back home but I had to stop and rest when the pain was too much. Then the baby came, I couldn't walk anymore, and I didn't know what to do. Finally an uncle came out looking for me when I didn't return. My grandmother had not realized my time was so close or she would not have let me go so far alone. They carried me back but I lost the baby. My grandmother took care of me so I recovered. Then she taught me all these things about what to do and how to take care of babies." (Delfina Cuero: *The Autobiography of Delfina Cuero,* as told to Florence Shipek pp 42–43)

The Sovereignty of Women

Control over production and the reproduction of human beings and all our relations is integral to sovereignty. It is this area of sovereignty which falls primarily in the domain of the female universe and encompasses the balances and forces which promote the harmony and well-being of the People. Women are the base of the generations. They are carriers of the culture. In many traditional societies, the children "belong" to the woman's lineage. Among the Iroquois, the Haudenosaunee, the women "owned" the gardens, and thereby controlled a major portion of the food supply. Supported by the Clan, the healers, and a community in harmony with the Creation, women had more to do with health than doctors are able to in today's fragmented world.

The concept of a universal "women's community" gives us the foundation with which to comprehend our physical and spiritual powers as women. What threatens the sovereignty of the women: of the women's community? What threatens the self-sufficiency of women in matters of production and reproduction, not just of human beings, but of all our relations upon which we depend for a healthy life? With the development of new and dangerous technologies affecting the control of women's cycles and female mechanical means of reproduction, it is more important now than ever to perceive what meanings lie in our existence as human beings and as Native women.

Everywhere we look, the measure of suffering for female life is the same. Reproduction for human beings and many of our relations is hardly a natural process. Chemicals, instruments, machines and distorted values sap the foundations of women's ways. Sterilization abuse, which has decimated the gene pool of less than a million Indians now in existence in the U.S., is a violation of Native women. Chemical contamination of our bodies and our environments is known to be the leading cause of high rates of cancer, genetic mutation and disease. On Pine Ridge reservation in South Dakota, 38% of the pregnant women suffered from miscarriages in one month in 1979. The miscarriage rate there is close to seven times greater than the U.S. national average.

In the not-too-long ago days and even still in some Indian communities, women were taught at puberty the things they needed to know to survive, physically and spiritually. These things were reflected in the songs, dances, various ceremonies, the everyday culture, in the stories the old ones told. For example, within the Iroquois social dances, the Woman's Dance is done to remind the women of their connection to the Mother Earth. We are an extension of Her. You look at the Earth and the old people will tell you that everything we need for a good life is provided for us by our common mother. Our laws, our education, our medicines, our religion, our food, shelter and clothing: everything came from the Earth, our Mother.

What are we doing as mothers to provide these things for our children? You look around in the Indian communities on the reservations and in the cities and you see how Indian women are losing their power on the female side of life. We have become more and more dependent on a way of life that does not belong to us. So dependent that breastfeeding, home births, parenting, and control over our own health and reproduction have become unfamiliar skills to us.

The consciousness of the Women's Dance, the awareness of our spiritual quality as women, and the concept of personal sovereignty, has to be the consciousness of our survival as women. We need to reclaim our powers on the female side of life.

Woman's Thread

I was born at home in 1952 in my grandmother's bedroom. I was the fourth child of a woman who had been told by doctors to not even have children because her heart suffered the damage of childhood rheumatic fever. Grandma delivered me and many of the children in my generation on the reservation at Akwesasne. I have been told that after I was born, I was placed in a basket next to my mother. Soon my grandmother walked by me and she noticed that my blanket was bloody. When she pulled it back, she saw that I was bleeding from the cord stump. Having raised 13 children of her own and having cared for so many others in the time of the Depression, Grandma was an excellent seamstress. So she took a needle and thread, sterilized it, and sewed up my navel. My brothers and sisters would always tease me as I was growing up, "You'd better not make Grandma mad or she's going to take her thread back!"

Grandma's large farm house sheltered her extended family through many passages in life. She delivered babies, held wedding receptions and funerals, and cared for family invalids. She was a one-woman institution. Her Mohawk name, Kanatires, means "she leads the village." Her beautiful quilts were sewn from the cast off clothing of her many children and grandchildren. In the way of old women, Grandma could not tolerate waste and she found a use for everything.

Grandma would rest in the evening, reading while she sat in her rocking chair. "Oh, Baby," she would sigh, and then she would go to her big iron bed that was separated only by a chintz curtain from where I slept. I remember thinking what a strange exclamation "Oh, baby" was for such an old woman whose only romance (although my sister and I would tease her about her occasional visits from Captain DeHollander) had died with my grandfather many years before. I carry the memory still of one such evening when my grandmother went to her bed to undress and put on her long flannel nightgown. I walked into her room and I saw her, sitting on the edge of the bed, naked to the waist, undressing. Her brown, wrinkled breasts sagged clear down to her waist. I was a young girl and I had never seen an old woman's breasts before. Grandma had felt my child's eyes upon her and she made no effort to hide herself, nor did she show any embarrassment, only an acknowledgment of my presence. At that moment I felt only a tremendous respect for this woman.

I spent a great deal of my childhood in my grandmother's care because of my mother's heart condition. I remember when my mother's exhausted heart had failed her for the final time, she was *waked* in the sitting room, next to my grandmother's bedroom where she had given birth so selflessly to me. I lay in my small bed and in the next room I could hear the old men sing Mohawk songs for my mother all night before they buried her. I was twelve then. That same spring, I had become a woman, or as they say in Mohawk, "her grandmother is visiting her." My mother's wish to live long enough to see her youngest child become a woman had been fulfilled. "Keep yourself clean here," she would say when she bathed me. "Someday a baby is going to come out of there." It had been strange how it happened when the blood came from between my legs for the first time. Ista (mother) was talking on the phone to an auntie about her upcoming open heart surgery, and as I passed by her on the way to the bathroom I could hear her say, "if only I could live long enough to see my baby become a woman." That is how it happened.

These are the women I come from and the spirit of their ways speaks to me still. My mother's heart, indestructible heart—she had survived long beyond her expected years out of pure love of a mother for her children—came to me last in a dream, bringing my daughter, Wahiahawi, to me three months before she would be born. I knew I would bear a girl and today I tell my daughter when I bathe her, "Keep yourself clean here, someday a baby is going to come out of there." My own mother's love is a source of strength to me as a mother.

Grandma delivered her last baby in 1953, her grandson Donald Louis. But she always kept her black bag of supplies on hand until she died in 1968. I remember how, after a series of strokes, death had claimed her slowly. Laboring to breathe, she was lying in a hospital bed inside an oxygen tent connected to a web of tubes. She was surrounded by the faces of her children and grandchildren. I touched her weathered hands that had worked so hard for so many all through her 83 years.

Grandma was drifting in and out of semiconsciousness. Suddenly she called for her husband who had died many years before. "Where's Louie?" she wanted to know. "The baby is almost here."

"My God, she thinks she's having a baby . . . we're here mother," my Uncle Noah comforted her.

In her final moments, as her family helped birth her into another world, Grandma's thoughts were of new life.

Grandma's nurturing breasts, withered melons whose roots did not die, gave new growth to me, her granddaughter (the Moon, after all, is our grandmother; she controls the cycles of all female life). When now, as a midwife myself, I see a woman's body yield to the emerging infant at childbirth, I too sometimes sigh, "Oh, Baby," and it is in these many small ways that I still carry my grandma's thread—the spirit that fuels the courage of my work.

Melanie M. Ellis

Through an art form, the best way I express myself is through creative writing. I was born into a military family on June 2nd, 1957. Am a graduate of the Institute of American Indian Arts High School in 1975. Later, in 1985, I graduated from the Institute of American Indian Arts, with an A.F.A. in creative writing.

My home is Oneida, Wisconsin. Currently I am serving a four year enlistment in the United States Navy, in Norfolk, Virginia.

Writing has taught me to understand myself. With this enlightenment, I am able to reach far more people by varying my styles and subject matter. Writing is a large part of me, like a skin I can not be without. If I coax an emotion, whether it be laughter, disgust, apathy or compassion, but an emotion, no matter what it is; then I know that I am successful.

The Farmhouse

Left the upstairs room that I shared with my three sisters, and crept along a narrow hallway. Mosquitos buzzed frantically, trying to escape through the humid, summer ceiling. Dumb insects! Didn't they know we always slept with the windows open? Gripped a banister rail to balance myself through pressing darkness.

Naked feet made the almond brown floor-boards creek in front of my brothers' open, yellow door. All three were asleep; one on the top bunk and two curled up on the bottom.

Every third stair would moan as my weight was felt upon it. Bong! Bong! Bong! The German grandfather clock couldn't sleep either. He stood there in the living-room, ticking our lives away. It always waited up for me on Saturday nights, keeping curfew company.

The braided rug was warm coils of footprints sifted into coarse fibers. It muffled soft cries from a wooded floor it covered. It filled the room comfortably, like the familiar scent of White Shoulders cologne.

Dad would still be awake in the stillness of his lair. A faint, red ember lit up now and again, becoming bright then dying. He emitted slow sighs of smoke. Those times when he lit his small cylinder of coals, night seemed to be at its darkest. Maybe, he was trying to discourage flying insects. Or, maybe he couldn't get use to sleeping alone.

Faint traces of spaghetti and bay leaves bantered in the kitchen, from a dinner eaten in another time. Wednesday night; spaghetti night. Cool linoleum crackled as I slipped inside the rectangular sun-porch.

Bong! [On the hour and once on the half hour.] You were the only thing that was constant, grandfather! You pulsed with the heart-beat of crickets, within your hard, green skin.

Six windows in a row, letting in star-light. Stars that held cold steel. Finally made the front door and whistled for my mongrel. He stretched, while crawling out from his favorite spot under the decaying aqua-blue and white trailer. Came and sat by me, and looked still half asleep. We listened to soft winds coming off the marsh, rustling cat-tails and pussy-willows.

No one awoke. No one knew of the escape. Crawled into bed beside my younger sister, Julie. Pulled flowered sheets up over my head, to try and drown out the mosquitos that still buzzed frantically, trying to escape through the humid, summer ceiling. Didn't they know we always slept with the windows open?

Ode: To an Indian Artist

I saw you on a poster once,
caressed by Taos Mountains.
You lingered in that dark age
with stars on your belt.
Dreams knew the name
you called yourself.
Like a new lithograph,
stretching inks enhanced corrupt
thoughts of Joy and love,
letting you fall blindly
into arroyos deeply
enmeshed through canyons.
You fermented so rapidly that year
with everything bottled inside.
Wine turned loose phantoms,
screaming through oils.
You lost your studio; the
only refuge left.
Going back to the place we met
you felt pieces of that crumbled world
trail behind; like flakes of mica, peeling.
You shattered inadequacies;
like a fist shatters glass.

Appaloosa Canyon

You stepped-out, on cool dunes.
  Blanket fluttering like some
lost bird's feathers.
  Black, faultless hair,
rising and falling; lazy sweet-grass smoke.
  I have summoned you
from the woodlands,
  where my people turn to trees.
Spirits beat their turtle-rattles
  on the rivers.
Your brothers sang in
  thunder-tongues, Horse-Woman.
Their meanings are imprisoned
  in the yellowness of sands.
(Can't you hear the Canyon
  when she's singing?)

Returning

Yesterday, two crows flew over me.
They asked what I was doing
all alone, way out there.
(They didn't tell me
any secrets of the air.)
A beaver walked with me
for some time.
We walked silently.
I could feel his strength,
saw his beauty.
For a beaver he was
well kept. As I watched
him slip into mist,
a tear fell from me
onto the road, and it
turned to ice for sorrow
is that cold. When I returned,
I searched for a pouch
that I'd left behind,
and I drew some tobacco
from its mouth. Upon burning it,
smoke streaked the air,
dancing about.

Ray Fadden / Tehanetorens

Mr. Fadden, recognized as an outstanding figure in Six Nations culture and history, was born in the Onchiota region of the Adirondack Mountains on August 23, 1910. From early childhood he has devoted his time to further the education of Indian children in the knowledge of their own history, traditions, and culture. While serving as an Indian instructor in a Boy Scout camp, he realized the great need of trained Indian counselors, qualified Indians, who could teach young white children the truth about early Indian history and the true character of the Indian people.

For twenty years Mr. Fadden was an instructor in Indian schools of the Six Nations. While at the Mohawk Indian School of Hogansburg, N.Y., he founded the Akwesasne Mohawk Counselor Organization, a youth club devoted to the teaching of Iroquois culture to the young people of the Six Nations. During its existence over three hundred young Indians received this training. Subjects included in the course were: bird and animal lore, camp craft, Indian ceremonials, Indian art and expression, Iroquois history, contributions of Indian peoples, first aid and physical culture. Club members visited other reservations, historical places, museums, and took part in many ceremonials and historical pageants.

Educators acknowledge their indebtedness to Ray Fadden for his contribution to American art, historical literature, and Indian culture.

—Julius Cook

Fourteen Strings of Purple Wampum to Writers About Indians

We hold in our hand fourteen strings of purple wampum. These we hand, one by one, to you – authors of many American history books; writers of cheap, inaccurate, unauthentic, sensational novels; and other writers of fiction who have poisoned the minds of young Americans concerning our people, the Red Race of America; to the producers of many western cowboy and Indian television programs and moving picture shows; to those Treaty-breakers who delight in dispossessing Indian Peoples by constructing dams on Indian lands in violation of sacred treaties; and to those of this, our country, who are prone to build up the glory of their ancestors on the bonds and life-blood of our Old People:

– With this first string of wampum, we take away the fog that surrounds your eyes and obstructs your view, that you may see the truth concerning our people!

– With this second string of wampum, we pull away from your imprisoned minds the cobwebs, the net that prevents you from dealing justice to our people!

– With this third piece of wampum, we cleanse your hearts of revenge, selfishness, and injustice, that you may create love instead of hate!

– With this fourth string of wampum, we wash the blood of our people from your hands, that you may know the clasp of true friendship and sincerity!

– With this fifth string of wampum, we shrink your heads down to that of normal man, we cleanse your minds of the abnormal conceit and love of self that has caused you to walk blindly among the dark people of the world.

– With this sixth string of wampum, we remove your garments of gold, silver, and greed, that you may don the apparel of generosity, hospitality, and humanity!

– With this seventh string of wampum, we remove the

dirt that fills your ears so you may hear the story and truth of our people!

— With this eighth string of wampum we straighten your tongues of crookedness, that in the future you may speak the truth concerning Indian People!

— With this ninth string of wampum, we take away the dark clouds from the face of the sun, that its rays may purify your thoughts, that you may look forward and see America, instead of backward toward Europe!

— With this tenth string of wampum, we brush away the rough stones and sticks from your path, that you may walk erect as the first American whose name you have defamed and whose country you now occupy!

— With this eleventh string of wampum, we take away from your hands your implements of destruction — guns, bombs, firewater, diseases — and place in them instead the Pipe of Friendship and Peace, that you may sow brotherly love rather than bitter hate and injustice!

— With this twelfth string of wampum, we build you a new house with many windows and no mirrors, that you may look out and see the life and purpose of your nearest neighbor, the American Indian!

— With this thirteenth string of wampum, we tear down the wall of steel and stone you have built around the TREE OF PEACE, that you may [take] shelter beneath its branches!

— With this fourteenth string of wampum we take from the hen-coop the eagle that you have imprisoned, that this noble bird may once again fly in the sky over America!

I, Te-ha-ne-to-rens, say this!

Migration of the Iroquois

This story is about the Hodenosaunee, as we say in our language, or the People of the Long House as it is translated into English, or the Iroquois as the French called us, or the Six Nations as the British called us.

Many winters in the past the Hodenosaunee lived toward the setting sun (west). They lived where the grass grew tall, and where the buffalo lived (The Great Plains). They lived beside the Great River (the Mississippi). The Iroquois lived toward the setting sun, where the grass grew tall, where the buffalo lived. They dwelt near the villages of the Wolf Nation (The Pawnees). They were friends and Allies of the Wolf Nation.

Northeast of their country were the Great Lakes. To the west rose the Rocky Mountains. Near the outlet of the Big River, the Mississippi, were the villages of the Hodenosaunee.

For some reason, the Iroquois packed their belongs on their backs and migrated. Many footmarks led away. They headed toward the rising sun. Up the Ohio River their trail went – toward the Great Lakes, they migrated toward the rising sun.

One band went across the Great Lakes and settled on Georgian Bay. They were known as the Thastchetchi, the Huron Nation. South of them settled the Tionontati, the Tobacco People. Another band settled along the shores of Lake Erie. They were the Gaguagaonon, the Erie People. Along the Niagara River settled the Hatiwatarunh, the neuter Nation. The Wenrohronon (Wenroe) Band settled southeast of the Neuters. Along the Susquehanna river settled the Kanastoge Nation. To the west of them, along the upper Ohio, the Honiasontkeronon (Black Minqua) built their towns. Up the Kanawha River migrated the Nottoway and Meherrin Peoples. Far to the south, across the Appalachian Mountains, migrated the Oyatageronon, the Cherokee People. One band went across the Great Lakes and settled in the north around Georgian Bay. They became known as the Huron Nation. One band went south through what is now known as Ohio and Kentucky. They crossed the Appalachian Mountains and settled in what is known as the Carolinas. They became the Cherokee Nation. The main band continued down the St. Lawrence River. There they met the Adirondack People.

The main band continued down the St. Lawrence River. There, they met a people who were different from them. These people were smaller physically than the Hodenosaunee, but there were more of them. They were hunters, while the Iroquois were more or less farmers. The Hodenosaunee noticed that when these people cooked their foods, they flavored them with different kinds of bark. So the Hodenosaunee called these people, "Adirondacks" or porcupines, meaning literally, the Eaters of Bark. The Iroquois did not get along well with the Adirondacks. Many battles were fought with the Bark Eaters. Because of this war there were many deaths. The Iroquois fought many battles with the Bark Eaters. In time, they were defeated by the Adirondacks. The Iroquois were defeated by the Bark Eaters. For many winters and many summers they, the Hodenosaunee, had to pay tribute of skins and meat to the Adirondack people, who had very good warriors. Darkness (sadness) filled the hearts of the People of the Long House. But the Hodenosaunee never forgot the Creator, and they continued to give thanksgiving to the plants, the waters, the sun, the moon, the animals, the winds. They wanted freedom, as the Eagle has. They—men, women, and children—continually spoke to the Creation and planned for freedom.

After many years of planning and with secretly-stored provisions, one dark night they left their village and silently paddled their canoes up the St. Lawrence River. Their water-trail led up this river, around the Thousand Islands, toward the mouth of the Oswego River. They looked back and saw specks on the water. These distant specks were the canoes of the Bark Eaters. The Hodenosaunee knew that the Adirondacks, not being burdened with women and children, had pursued them and would reach them before they could land.

The Adirondacks overtook the Iroquois near the mouth of the Oswego River. A great battle took place. For a time, it looked as if the Iroquois would be wiped out. The Thunder People heard their cry of distress and sent a great storm. In the confusion, the rough waters and high winds, many of the canoes of the Adirondacks overturned. Those who survived returned home.

Near the mouth of the Oswego River, the Hodenosaunee landed and erected their village. They found good hunting. They found a rich soil, good for the raising of corn, beans and squash. For many years the home fires of the People of the Long House burned and their bark houses stood near the Oswego River. In time, they multiplied. There were many men, women, and children. The game, being used for food, became scarce.

Finally, different bands of Hodenosaunee left the homeland seeking better hunting regions. They were looking for signs of deer. From their homeland along the Oswego River, their trails led south, east, and west. The Flint People, who are called by others the Mohawks, settled along the Mohawk River. Around Oneida Lake, the Standing Stone People, or Oneidas, built their villages. The People of the Hills, or Onondagas, settled along Onondaga Creek. To the west, along Cayuga Lake, the Great Pipe People, or Cayugas, built their towns. Along Canandaigua Lake settled the People of the Great Mountain, the Senecas. Another band, the Akotaskarore, or Tuscaroras, travelled far to the south. Now they, the one band, had become six separate bands. To the east was the Hudson River, running to the sea. To the west stretched the Great Lakes and the St. Lawrence River. North was the Adirondack Mountain region and south were the Finger Lakes. In time, although related by blood, the five nations who remained in the north, became enemies of each other. They forgot the ways of the Creator, and fought among themselves and with others, bringing sorrow, destruction and death to each nation.

Two wise men, one whom we call today the Peacemaker, and Aiionwentha, organized the five nations of Long

House People into a confederacy. The Peacemaker gave them a government and constitution to follow, called Kaianeregowa, or the Great Nice Way. Today we often call it "the Great Law".

The Peacemaker said, "To war against each other is foolish as well as evil. Hunters are afraid to seek game in the forests. Fishermen fear to follow the streams. Women are afraid to work in the fields. Because of war, there is starvation, suffering, and misery. War must cease and everlasting Peace must be established among all peoples." The warriors of the Five Nations listened and thought of the words of the Wise One. They threw down their weapons of war.

The Five Nations of the People of the Long House allied themselves into one League. They compared themselves to a long bark house, where there would be five fireplaces, but all were of one family. The Flint People, the Mohawks, were the Keepers of the Eastern Door of that Long House. The Senecas were Keepers of the Western Door. The Onondagas, in the center, were the Fire Keepers, and theirs became the capitol of the League.

The Five Nations became as brothers again. They worked together as one people. If any one of these nations were attacked, the injury was felt by all of the Five Nations.

The Rotiianeson, or Nice People, whom some today call "chiefs", contributed white wampum toward a Great White Circle of Wampum. This wampum circle is the symbolic Fire of the Great Council which burns at Onondaga. It certifies the pledge words of the Rotiianeson that they will keep the unity of the Confederacy, that they are united, and form one body or League of Great Peace, which they have established. The fifty strings of wampum facing the center represent the Rotiianeson, fifty in number, the Government of the Five Nations. Each string stands for one of our leaders, and they are placed in the order in which they sit at council.

This sacred wampum belt symbolizes the union of the Five Nations. It was made to remember the Great Peace. It means: the Five Nations are joined together by the Path of Peace. In the center is a white heart, symbolizing the Onondaga nation. It also means that the heart of the

Five Nations is single in its loyalty to the Great Peace, and that the Great Peace is lodged in the heart, with the Onondaga people. The Peace Path extends beyond at both ends, meaning that others may follow this path, and become part of the Great Peace, Kaianerekowa.

The Peacemaker said, "Our League is a Great Tree. It reaches high into the sky so that all peoples will see and know of it. The Eagle watches from its top as our guardian bird. The Tree has four white roots, White Roots of Peace that go to the four winds. If any man or any nation shall show a desire to trace these roots to their source and obey the Law of the Great Peace, they shall be made welcome to take shelter beneath this tree." Many nations took shelter beneath this tree, becoming a part of the first United Nations. Weapons of war are buried deep in the earth.

For many years, the Iroquois Confederacy guarded and protected the Thirteen Colonies from invasion from the north. If it had not been for this protection during the several French and English Wars, it would not have been possible for the United States of America to begin.

Also, white leaders watched the operation of the Iroquois government and learned union and democracy from it. Historians are now beginning to admit what they must have known a long time ago – that the government of the United States is not patterned after something across the ocean, where they believed in the divine right of kings and where the people had no voice, but it is patterned after the government of the people of the Long House, where all people – women as well as men – are represented and control their government.

If any foreign nation insisted upon war to gain its ends, it was always warned three times in open council to obey the Law of the Great Peace and settle its disputes by talking them over. If after the third warning, that nation insisted upon force, it got no other chance. The War Belt was thrown at its feet, and the Five Nations fought it until it was conquered. Their people were not killed or tortured, but were adopted by the Five Nations, assigned lands, and were given the same rights and privileges as other Iroquois. The only freedom they lost was the freedom to wage war.

Because of the Great Law, Kaiianerekowa, the sun shone strong in the hearts of the native peoples of this land. They were a happy people when they lived in America under the Tree of Peace.

The Gift of the Great Spirit

The old Iroquois told this story to the young people to teach them to be kind to the aged.

Many Winters and Summers in the past *(arrow going back)* there was an Iroquois village. One day, an old man appeared at the edge of this village. The old man wore ragged clothes. He seemed very tired and looked hungry. As he walked through the village he looked over the door of each house. Over the doors of the bark houses were the emblems of the clans of those who occupied the lodges. The old man came to a lodge on which was hung a Turtle shell. Turtle Clan members lived in this house. He pulled the door curtain, and asked for food and night's lodging. He was refused by the woman of the house. He was told to move on. Going on his way, he soon came to a house with a snipe skin over the door. When he asked for food he was again told to move on. Thus he traveled to houses belonging to the Wolf, Beaver, Deer, Eel, Heron, and Eagle Clans. At each house he was treated with scorn, and told to move on.

At length, tired and weary, the old man came to the edge of the village. He saw a little bark house. Hanging over the door of this house was a carved bear's head. It was a house of the Bear Clan. An old woman came out of the house. When she saw how tired the stranger looked, she asked him to enter her lodge, that he was welcome to what little she had. She gave him food to eat. She spread soft deer skins and asked him to rest his tired body. The next day, the man sickened and came down with a fever.

He told the woman to go into the forest and . . . gather a certain kind of plant. He instructed her how to prepare the plant and to make a certain kind of medicine. After taking the medicine, the old man recovered. The old man became ill on many different days. Each time that he was ill, it was from a different kind of sickness. With each illness, he sent the old woman into the forest to gather different kinds of herbs. Each time that the old woman returned with the herbs, the old man gave her instructions on how to prepare and make a medicine of the herb for each kind of sickness that he had. When he drank the medicine, he recovered.

One day, the old woman was about to enter her home when she saw a great light shining in her lodge. Upon looking up, she saw a handsome young man standing at the entrance of her bark house. His face shone like the sun. Her heart was filled with fear. She was frightened. She thought that a spirit stood before her. The young man said, "Fear not, good woman. I am the Creator. I came to the lodges of the Iroquois in the form of an old man.

"I wandered from house to house asking for food and shelter.

"I asked for food and shelter of the Turtle Clan, Snipe Clan, Wolf Clan, Beaver Clan, Deer Clan, Eel Clan, Heron Clan and Eagle Clan. Each time I was refused food and shelter and told to move on.

"Only you, of the Bear Clan, sheltered and fed me. For that reason, I have taught you cures for all of the sickness known to the Real People. Many times I became ill. Many times, I sent you into the forest to gather herbs. I told you how to make medicine from the herbs. When I took of this medicine, I recovered from my illnesses.

"From this day on, the Medicine Men and Women will always belong to the Bear Clan.

"They, Bear Clan members, will be the Keepers of the Medicine for all time to come."

Needles

There was a little Indian boy at Akwesasne. His name was Joe Brown. He lived on Racquette Road. One day Joe come to school with a little porcupine, just a baby. He still had quills even though he was very small. I said Joe, you should never take a little animal away from its mother. That animal's mother loves that little porcupine just as much as your mother cares for you. That's a cruel thing you did taking that baby away from its mother. He said, "Mr. Fadden, I didn't take it away. I was in the woods, Fulton's woods, and he was on the log. And I looked all around for the mother and he must have been lost, so I took it home." Well, I said, I realize now that you didn't mean to do this, but now I've told you, whenever you find a little raccoon or porcupine in the woods, any baby animal, just leave him alone. The mother knows where he or she is. The mother will take a little porcupine, put him on a stump, and tell him not to move, stay right there. Then she goes off in the woods, she eats leaves and bark, and forages around. She can tell by the way her breast feels, when it's time to feed the little one. She makes a noise. The little one, it has good ears. They come together, he eats his dinner, he follows the mother. I said, how long ago did you pick that little fellow up? "A day and a half ago." Ahh, I said, it's too late. She's already come, and she thinks somebody killed her baby. She's probably crying inside. I said, it's too bad but we'll have to bring it up right here in school. We'll have to give him a name. So, what do you suppose we call him? Needles. Because he had a lot of little needles.

Even though he was a baby porcupine, he wasn't afraid of us. He figured we were his mother. He was so small he couldn't get a bottle nipple in his mouth. We had to feed him with an eyedropper. We warmed the milk, put a little sugar in, and then you fed him. The only trouble is, he eats every three hours, all night long. I used to take him home with me. He stayed under the kitchen sink. When I first brought him home I let him sleep right on the bed. Well, 10:00 at night he starts calling. Just like a little kid calling for something to eat. What are you going to do? I warmed the milk and I'd feed him. Then he'd go back to sleep again. Three hours later, all over again. Three hours later, all over again. I was glad when he started to eat out of a dish. And him and my dog got along okay. They got along fine.

When Needles was a little baby, and he did his business on the floor, it wasn't too bad. He was just a baby. But when he got to weigh 30 pounds, and he did it on the floor, phew, what a smell. You know that stuff that you wash things with? Ammonia they call it, it makes your eyes smart. So my wife said, "You're going to teach him to do that on paper or he's going out." So just like training a dog, every time he did it, I'd pick him up like a cat, put his nose in it, and then put him on the paper. Believe it or not, I taught him to do it on the paper. Then I'd burn the paper. But I didn't get downwind from it.

He knew how to open the door and he slept under the kitchen sink. When he got full grown, I taught him how to open the back door. I figured he was getting big enough to be on his own. So I'd let him loose and follow him. You know how slow a porcupine is, he didn't know I was following him. He always headed for the hill behind my house because there was a female porcupine up there. I don't know how he knew, but there was one up there.

One day Needles stood in front of the kitchen door, and he was going back and forth. I told my wife, this is cruel. I said, we could treat him and give him all the food in the world, but he wants to be free. I said, an eagle, he may be starving up in the sky, but he would rather starve to death than to be put in a hen coop and be made a chicken out of him. Let's let him go and pray he doesn't walk up to some human being, and pray he doesn't get hit by a car. So this one time, I didn't follow him. I opened the back door and he waddled down the steps, and he disappeared into the woods.

My wife and I, we couldn't sleep. He was like our kid, you know. We loved him. I went walking up and down the road with my flashlight thinking he might come down the road. My wife told me to sleep out on the porch. I said he can open the door. She answered, "Sleep out on the porch!" She's the boss, I sleep out on the porch. During the night, I heard gnawing. You know, if you put salt on a stump, the porcupines chew the stump and leave your house alone. I placed the light over there, looked at the porcupine; I looked close, but it wasn't Needles. Three other porcupines came during the night. No Needles. Meanwhile, no sleep.

It was just getting light in the east, when I looked down the trail, and there came Needles just as fast as his fat legs could carry him. I said "Needles!" with happiness in my voice. He just glanced at me, rushed right by me, rushed to the steps, rushed up the steps, rushed across the porch, rushed to the door, opened the door with a slam, and rushed to the paper. He held it all night in the woods. It's a true story. I put paper all the way across the kitchen floor and he took it all before he was through.

Well, they always said you should start a talk with a funny story. There you have it, except it is all true.

Stephen Fadden

Much of my inspiration to work as a communicator, as a writer and as a storyteller, has come from my family. My parents and siblings have been tremendously supportive of my work, and much of my Ongwe-oweh knowledge and pride has been given to me by my uncle Ray Tehanetorens Fadden and cousin John Kahionhes Fadden.

I am preparing to become an eco-journalist, a warrior with words. Our world has reached a critical time, when journalists must become subjective in their viewpoints, to call global attention to the destruction of our Earth Mother. Ongwe-oweh, and many other tribal peoples have a way of looking at the natural order of things, reverent and respectful of our dependence on all the things of creation. It is this kind of thinking that motivates me now. Poems and stories are beautiful and necessary, but without the natural world – water, air, animals and green things – to base our prose upon, our words and lives are meaningless. This work I must do, not only for Ongwe-oweh, but for all people, plants and animals.

Gifts of the Maple

Leader Tree Of The Woodlands

Maple sugar festivals have become a yearly tradition in many small towns in Upstate New York, serving as social functions for people to congregate, celebrate and exchange greetings and stories from the previous year. The tradition of a maple festival is not a new one in the northeastern United States and Canada, where maple sugar season signals the reawakening of green life after the winter season. The month when the sap flows has for centuries been a special time of year to native peoples of the northeastern American continent, for maple syrup is the first plant resource, even before wild strawberries, that humans can harvest when the winter snows start to subside.

The strength of a maple sugar tradition is found in the native oral record. No written or physical documentation of Native American people descriptive of ancient activities involving maple sugar is available, however. Conversely, the description of maple activity is virtually absent from the European record until after contact with New World peoples. The wealth of references to the Native American sugar harvest practices is to be found in early journals of visitors to the New World and is also documented in numerous anthropological records.

Among the Iroquois, the Maple Festival is the first of six thanksgivings performed throughout the year, done with a reverent, yet festive air of ancient custom. O? tadihno:nyo:? neh wahda? — "They give thanks to the maple" — is mentioned in the ancient Iroquois Thanksgiving Address, an oral tradition that is still used to begin and conclude important meetings.

Lewis Henry Morgan, who wrote *League of the Iroquois* in 1851, drew heavily on the knowledge of the Seneca, Ely S. Parker, when he reported that the maple thanksgiving was one that the Iroquois evidently celebrated since ancient times and were obligated to do so every season. Ironically, Morgan still posed the question in his book's footnotes about whether the Iroquois learned the maple sugaring practice from whites or vice-versa. Morgan, a Rochester lawyer known in some circles as "the father of American anthropology," might have been the progenitor of the idea that the Iroquois, "for want of suitable vessels among them for boiling," learned the practice from Europeans.

Dr. Arthur C. Parker, a Seneca man who worked for the Rochester Museum of Arts and Sciences, in his monograph *The Iroquois Uses of Maize*, wrote, "The maple tree started the year. Its returning and rising sap to the Indian was the sign of the Creator's renewed covenant." Parker, and several other anthropologists, noted that a tradition exists among the Iroquois that long ago, before European contact, the Iroquois migrated from where the Mississippi, Missouri and Ohio rivers came together. The main band of Iroquois eventually moved to the northern woodland areas of New York state, where they encountered a group of forest people they called the Adirhondaks. The name roughly meant "bark eaters" and was used in recognition that these people flavored their foods with the barks of certain trees. It might be a reasonable speculation that the Iroquois learned about making maple syrup from the Adirhondaks. A prominent part of this migration story attests that the Iroquois fell into conflict with the Adirhondaks, were defeated and were made into a tribute-surrendering nation. The tradition also states that the Iroquois made their break for freedom after the women threw boiling hot maple sap into the faces of the Adirhondak warriors, allowing the Iroquois families to make good their escape.

The mention of maple sugaring is widely reported in the journals of early European travelers on the North American continent. The first documented reference to maple sugar was by an English author, in a book by Robert Boyle, published in 1664. Boyle said he was told by the natives of New England about a tree that exudes a saccharine sap. Another early reference to making maple sugar can be found in the late 1690's journal of Sebastian Rasles, a missionary to the Abenaki: "It is curious to note that the method of extracting the bayberry wax and making maple sugar, articles of considerable importance to us, has been learned of the aborigines."

Yet, some historians have cited a lack of adequate native technology to harvest maple sugar and imply the maple sugaring tradition came from European origins. Among many Native American groups, the tradition of maple processing in America is said to pre-date European contact. An early traveler along the St. Peter's River once raised the question of maple syrup origin to a Kickapoo man, who succinctly retorted in effect, "Can it be that you are so simple as to ask me such a question, seeing that the Master of Life has given us minds that enable us to substitute stone hatchets for those made of steel by the whites; and we should not know as well as they how to manufacture sugar? He has made us all, that we should enjoy life; he has placed before us all of the needs for existence, wherefore then should he have withheld from us the art of excavating the trees in order to make troughs of them, of placing the sap in these, of heating the stones and throwing them into the sap to make it boil and reduce it to sugar?"

The Kickapoo man described a culturally-rooted fondness of maple sugar and the essence of sugar making using the available tools, and chastised the traveler for his insinuation that the native people were not astute enough to discover and harvest nature's gifts. According to several early European observers, the incredibly simple process, using the natural world-relevant technology of native peoples, was effective enough to generate a surplus of sugar products that were used in trade transactions with other tribes. The sugar making techniques, more likely, were mimicked by Europeans, who in turn made maple sugar a delicacy of high demand in Europe. Robert Beverly's 1705 book, *History and Present State of Virginia*, provided his observations of Native American maple sugaring: "The sugar-tree yields a kind of sap or juice, which by boiling is made into sugar. This juice is drawn out, by wounding the trunk of the tree, and placing a receiver under the wound. The Indians make one pound of sugar out of eight pounds of the liquor. Though this discovery has not yet been made by the English by above twelve or fourteen years; it has been known among the Indians longer than any now living can remember."

If European modes of sugar reduction, which entailed the employment of copper kettles, metal spiles and iron evaporating vats were taught to Native American people, it should logically follow that Indians would have used the exact same modes and tools to replicate the process.

The maple syrup technology used by Native Americans was simple, and according to Dr. David Bates, of Cornell University's College of Agriculture and Life Sciences, the ancient native process has been successfully replicated in modern times, using the same types of materials. In order to draw the sap from the tree, a vertical slash was cut in the tree, about two inches deep, one foot long and three to four feet above the ground. Reeds, shingles or concave slabs of bark were then driven into the bottom of the slash to run the sap from the gash into a container. The sap was gathered in pots made of birch bark, in bowls of hollowed out wood or in clay pots that had cracked from excessive heat. If bark was used, the slabs would be grooved and folded to prevent breakage and the seams were sealed with resin. Most buckets could hold one or two gallons of raw fluid. A large tree could yield three to six pounds of sugar per year. The sap was reduced to sugar by heating fire-formed stones until they were red hot and then the stones were dropped into the vat of raw sap, which caused the sap to boil and evaporate. The technique, by modern standards, might seem crude and tedious, but is ingenious nonetheless.

Another less tedious method of maple sugar processing involved running the sap into containers and allowing the sap to freeze in the collecting containers overnight. In the morning the ice would be removed and boiled down and the remaining thick syrup collected.

The sugar maple, silver maple, wild cherry, black maple, box elder, birch and ash trees have been recorded as sugar-yielding resources for Native American people.

The syrup was often used to season bread, beans, squash, meat or was mixed with pounded parched corn to be used as a highly nourishing and compact food for long journeys. Maple sugar has often been said to have no equal in the New World for flavor and nutrition. A small sack of the corn and maple sugar mixture could carry a man for one or two months on the road, remarked Peter Kalm in his 1837 book, *A Journey Into North America.* One Jesuit missionary wrote about Iroquois pouring the syrup over popcorn, naming it "snowfood." Another technique of processing the raw syrup was to boil it long enough so that when it cooled, the liquid would harden into granulated crystals. The hot syrup would then be poured into empty duck and quail eggs or poured into bark molds.

The maple tree also had medicinal uses among Native American peoples as an astringent (with its products employed for the chemical ability to shrink tissues and check the flow of blood by contracting blood vessels), deobstruent (remove blockages from vital organs), and a tonic. Among the Iroquois, a decoction of boiled leaves and bark was used by many for relief of liver and spleen problems, and a decoction of inner bark was used as an eye wash. Maple sugar added to boiling water sometimes was used to soothe stomach ailments. A poultice of boiled leaves and tea was used for boils. The internal uses of maple products include cough medicine, expectorant, diuretic, and anti-diarrheal.

The maple tree has far-reaching implications on the religious, social and cultural motivations of Native Americans in the woodland areas. The tree has been a rich source of food and medicine as long as the human mind can remember, and for these two gifts, the maples are still honored and revered. The respect given to the maple is well-illustrated by Tom Porter, of the Akwesasne Mohawk Nation, who said recently, "The maple, in our part of the world, is the Master of the tree life. The maple is the elder."

Germaine General-Myke

My name is Germaine General-Myke. I am an Onondaga/Cayuga Indian of the wolf clan. I was born on the Six Nations Reserve in Ohsweken, Ontario. My parents were Alexander and Ida General, both deceased in 1965.

I was raised in the traditional mode of the Longhouse faith. At the age of ten and knowing no English nor my given name, I was enrolled at School #1, on the reserve. My sister and I were later transferred to School #2, in the village of Ohsweken. The distance to school was two miles each way. I dropped out of school in the eighth grade at the age of sixteen. Since leaving home at twenty to go to work, the city of Buffalo has been home.

Married in 1956, and widowed in 1973, my marriage blessed me with four wonderful daughters, and am a Nana to ten beautiful grandchildren.

From 1975 to 1983, I was a volunteer editor for a Native American Indian Newsletter, in which a few of my writings were published. I love writing but time does not allow me the pleasure to devote to it. I started writing at the age of twelve, but my grammar was so poor I was ashamed and would destroy the copies as soon as written – a habit even in later years yet to be amended.

In 1978, I enrolled in an Adult Learning Center, and within the same year received my GED. Then in 1983, D'Youville College was offering a Short Story Course to which I applied and was accepted. I completed one semester and earned three credits. However, in securing a job that proved too demanding, I had to deter my educational pursuits.

My love of knitting, crocheting, writing, walking, and horticulture is only surpassed by my enthusiasm for watching hockey and attending lacrosse games.

Maple Trees

Nature sounding its cycle
The frozen bed of the pond
Giving way to the warmth all around
Listening to the sound like raindrops
Making music on dead leaves
The realization is overwhelming
It is time for the syrupy liquids to flow
And there is nothing there to catch it
The maple trees are weeping
Taking one quick stride toward it
Embracing tightly to the tree
Then moving underneath the branches
To catch some of the tear drops
Tasting the moistness, its sweetness
Leaving the woods and still hearing
Joined by the birds singing
There's music in the woods today
The maple trees are weeping.

Dehgruh Niwase Ahseh

Ah hee, Auh ghee,	I thought, I'd say,
Ah gut senooni,	I am glad,
Swa gway ghonh	All of you
A gwa geh,	I see,
Dis wah tres,	All came forth,
Nan tho, Wahnay.	Here, today.
Ees a sa tune deh,	You have heard,
Ees aw sut town siyos,	You have listened,
Odeh oom gwa	What we
Troh wi.	Spoke of.
Nan tho,	Here,
Ha dinna greh au sooh,	They live still,
Nay Hodennoshoni,	The People of the Longhouse,
Nah gih:	They are:
O neh yoht ga,	Oneida,
Da gay ga,	Onondaga,
Deh wa ga,	Seneca,
Ga yen khono,	Mohawk,
Go yo kono,	Cayuga,
Tho gih wa hey	And I just
Sooh ga sa,	Remembered,
Dus goweh, nih.	Tuscarora, too.
Nya Weh	Thank You

Reservation

(Six Nations)

The speed of sound has reached the Rez
As I found to my dismay
Used to be such bliss
Visiting the old home town as they say
Now remnants of ease exist
Houses of grandeur now stand
Where once there was bushy land
The speed of modernization
Has overtaken most of the Nations
What will become, where has the indian time gone?
Might be back in the city from whence I come.

To see, feel and smell the Rez all around
Glancing and barely seeing the auto passing
I should know that face that is a blur
Yes, the pace on the Rez is hastening
Has taken with some lives I hear
Distant and some relatives dear
The easy tempo of living on the Rez
May some day be a memory gone past
Oh, how I wish that it will last
Indian people sure have grown
Their number that is still unknown.

A prophecy one way foretells
But no one listens to that kind of sell
It grieves me more, the young die young
In the city and on the Rez
Missing the growing pain of joy
Whether it be a girl or a boy
Coasting hills and climbing trees
Running carefree in the fields
Bingo, lacrosse and ice games to volley ball
Shouts of education now fill the hall

And Native youngsters must survive.

Something of value is amiss
Native people are happy today
What unheard voices there are to say
Some unpaved roads of dust hug the air
Where once earthy dust touched the ground
Could it be then once a dream
To be born and raised there on the Rez?
Will the people wake one day
And see the reservation gone away?

Come Spring

With the soft awakening
Of Mother Earth
From a long winter's rest
The comforting warmth
Of Mother Earth rises
To spread fragrances
Across many lands
To many nations, welcome
The south wind
Its strength, its freshness,
From Big Brother, the sun
Who ascends in the east
Greeting our Grandfathers
The Thunderers
With their cleansing of rain
Coming from the west
There Grandmother Moon
With her bright sweet face
Surveys the happenings
On the body of Mother Earth
Many nod in unison
In existing partnership
With our Creator above
As once again
All creatures stir in their abode,
Are enfolded in the arms
Of the Creator's love.

Hill

Richard Hill

I was born in Buffalo, NY in 1950 to a family of Ironworkers and hunters. My father was an Ironworker for over 35 years and my brothers and I also worked as Ironworkers for the Buffalo Local.

I then went to art school at the Art Institute of Chicago to study photography from 1968 to 1971. Returning to Buffalo, I began a career as a photographer for local museums and completed a photo survey of Iroquois artists and craftspeople for the New York State Historical Society in 1971.

I was awarded a fellowship by the America the Beautiful Fund to create a series of watercolor paintings of Iroquois culture. A meeting with Ernie Smith of Tonawanda greatly influenced my early work to document Native American culture. I later was awarded a C.A.P.S. fellowship to continue my creative painting.

In 1973 I worked with an artist's committee to organize an "Exhibition of Iroquois Arts and Crafts" for the Everson Museum of Art in Syracuse. Since that time I have curated over twenty art exhibits and currently I serve on a committee for a major traveling exhibit that is scheduled to open in Japan next year.

I have also prepared several museum exhibits on Iroquois Indians for the Buffalo Historical Society, the Smithsonian Institution, the Native American Center for the Living Arts, and the "Skywalkers – History of Indian Ironworkers" exhibit for the Woodland Indian Culture Centre of Brantford, Ontario.

In the past I have been the Museum Director of the Turtle; Director of the North American Indian Museums Association; Manager of the Indian Art Centre, Ottawa, Ontario; Design Consultant for Ganondagan State Park, Victor, NY.

Currently I am the Art Director of DAYBREAK, a national newsmagazine, and an Instructor in American Studies for the State University of New York at Buffalo.

I have written for many publications, including Four Winds Journal, American Indian Art Magazine, History News, Museum News, Outdoor Educator, Lacrosse Magazine, Muse, Northeast Indian Quarterly, and the Turtle Quarterly.

My interests are photography, traditional arts, Iroquois history, lacrosse, and visual arts. I occasionally paint watercolor and acrylic paintings, however my writing and design work occupies most of my time.

I have seven children, three dogs, five cats and two cars that take turn not running.

Skywalkers

Tradition is often hard to isolate for the hodinoso:ni* and the Woodland Indians of the Northeast. To some, tradition is doing things the "old ways", following the time honoured steps of the elders of our communities. To others, tradition is a way of thinking, of showing respect for the values and spirituality of our ancestors, in spite of the way we live today. And to others, tradition is whatever is handed down from one gener-

---

*hodinoso:ni   When referring to themselves, Iroquoians used the name, hodinoso:ni. The literal meaning is "house builders." This symbolic word is derived from the political structure when the Great Law was given to the Iroquois by the Creator. It is analogous to an Iroquoian longhouse, a structure erected piece by piece. If one part is removed the building cannot stand. As a result of the symbolic structure, the Great Law retains its religious significance to the Iroquois. (Reg Henry, Personal Communication, 26 July 1987)

ation to the next. To most, it is what we learn from our family that makes tradition a viable tool for dealing with the future. All these definitions come to play in describing the role of the Ironworker among the Woodland Indians of Canada and the U.S.

Ironwork is an extension of the traditions of our ancestors. Mohawk men have been Ironworkers for over one hundred and thirty years. Ironwork, like other cultural traditions, inspires values of self-worth, and gives the Indian men a significant and courageous role in the contemporary world.

"Son follows father," reflected Stoney Isaacs, Business Agent for Hamilton Local 736 of the International Association of Bridge, Structural and Ornamental Iron Workers. Indeed, most of the Indian Ironworkers that I interviewed for this exhibit said that it was their father, brother, uncle or some other relative that broke them into the profession of Ironwork. My father raised his sons to be Ironworkers, it was just the thing to do; it was following in your family's footsteps. Family has remained important to Indian Ironworkers.

The tradition of Ironwork has spread over several generations of Woodland Indians, and has begun to impact on the lives of Native People across North America. The National Ironworkers Training Program for American Indians of Broadview, Illinois has trained over 570 Indians from across the States, including several Indian women. The program graduates about 40 new Ironworkers each year. There are 153,151 Ironworkers in the International Union, of which about only 7,500 are Indians. Yet, Ironwork is one of the main occupations of the Woodland Indians.

Ironwork is more than just a way to make a living to the Woodland Indians. Construction is a Woodland Indian tradition itself. Look at the ancient "Sky Cities" of the Mound Builders that still stand after several thousand years. Ironworkers perform a very ancient skill — they build structures, not unlike their ancestors who built 200 foot long longhouses. Don't forget that the Iroquois call themselves hodinoso:ni — meaning "They build longhouses." Building is part of our tribal identity. Ironworkers have become the builders of long bridges and tall lodges of the modern world.

Ironwork is a traditional activity because it also fulfills a social and cultural need in our communities. Ironworkers of today, like the traders and trappers of the past, travel great distances seeking the advantage of the next job, and secure goods for their families back home. For men, Ironwork provides an immediate opportunity to prove yourself, to show your skills and to gain respect of others. Such opportunity allows the men to develop a lot of self-confidence. Ironworkers are providers, a traditional role for men.

The myth of the Ironworker places an inborn sense of balance in all Indians, some kind of genetic equilibrium that allows the Indian Ironworker to stick to steel the way a mountain goat clings to a steep cliff. That myth is shattered each time an Indian falls from the lifeless steel, and fall they do. My father and brother both fell. Most Ironworkers have fallen at least once. All know someone who was killed on the job.

If there is anything innate to Indian Ironworkers it is their desire to prove themselves, to show their nerve and agility. But most of all, they want to show their pride in a job well done.

The success of the Indian Ironworker is based upon both family upbringing and personal ambitions, not solely upon sure-footed genes. Ironwork is not for all Indians; many have tried and quit. Many have only admired the skill of the Ironworker from afar. Some Indians are even afraid of hard work. Yet, what is it that seems to make Indians such good Ironworkers? What makes an Indian walk out on a narrow beam, high in the air, to build the white man's world? Why do Indian Ironworkers, who come from communities where there are not tall buildings, like to work on the top? Most importantly, what makes a man get up and climb back on the steel after he has fallen?

Construction Is Our Tradition

Indian people have been reshaping their environment to build shelter for their families, to protect their villages and to express their sacred concerns. Modern architects and engineers are just beginning to recognize the true value of construction techniques of Native People across North America. The Pueblo peoples of the Southwest constructed elaborate apartment complexes and underground chambers that have remained for thousands of years. Much of the modern architecture of the Southwest is based upon these ancient models.

The Northwest Coast peoples constructed huge houses of cedar and made the world's largest single-piece sculptures in their totem poles. They also constructed catwalk bridges across the deep ravines as well as pole towers from which they could spear salmon.

The Plains peoples constructed huge circular "Earth Lodges" of large poles, covered with sod. These dwellings were up to 50 feet in diameter and were arranged in permanent villages.

Among Woodland cultures, construction also plays a prominent role. The Iroquois and the Huron were noted for their grand longhouses, some up to 300 feet long. Their early villages were so extensive that the europeans called them "castles" and "forts." Champlain made detailed sketches of the Mohawk towns that he confronted in the 17th century, showing double palisaded walls, dozens of longhouses, and defensive catwalks. Some Woodland villages contained over 100 longhouses, inhabited by an estimated 5,000 villagers.

Cartier described the Mohawk village of Hochelaga along the St. Lawrence in 1556 as a settlement of fifty longhouses, surrounded by triple palisades. Rev. Samual Kirkland describes the Seneca town of Tegataenedaghgwe in 1790 as a double fortified town, with two round palisades at each end, four acres in diameter. The entire town was two miles long.

Such communities took much planning and cooperative labour. Fields would have to be cleared, logs would have to be prepared and each building would have to be raised by hand. Villages would be occupied for 15 to 20 years, and then would be moved to a new location, at times, only 20 miles upstream. The whole process of construction would begin again.

The task of construction is nothing new to the Woodland Indians. This can account for the acceptance of Ironwork and other construction trades as an important occupation among the Woodland Indians of today. Whereas construction and farming were the principal activities of the ancient Indian cultures, Ironwork has become the common denominator of the Iroquois people of the modern era.

Bridge building is also a Native skill. We can find many examples of aboriginal structures to cross rivers from British Columbia to Ontario. The Iroquois actually had a foot bridge tradition that remained into the 1950's. A wooden foot bridge at Tonawanda Seneca Indian Reservation was recalled by Corbett Sundown, Seneca Chief. He remembered crossing the bridge as a kid, and marveled at the fact that it was made entirely of wood, with no nails or wire. He felt that the technology for such a bridge was very ancient.

Even with the introduction of the log cabin, the Woodland Indians continued their construction excellence. 18th-century Iroquois villages adapted new technology to produce some of the best-made homes on the frontier. A case in point is the Seneca town of Kanadesaga, which was the capital of the Seneca Nation in central New York. It was the largest town at that time, comprised of 72 log cabins, laid out in a circular form, surrounding a central green. The village was complete with a two story home, trading post and blacksmith shop. Some of the Seneca homes had split log floors, stone fireplaces and Dutch ovens. In 1779 Col. Gansevoort wrote "those Indians live much better than most of the Mohawk River farmers, their houses were well furnished . . . "

Woodland Indians have a tradition of construction, of building cities and large buildings. Ironwork follows closely to that tradition, not only in the technology, but in the nature of the work. Hard work is also an Indian tradition. Cooperative labour is an important part of aboriginal societies, and men and women had ample opportunity to work collectively to the benefit of their communities.

Adventure Is Also Our Tradition

Ironwork is hard, challenging work, requiring the body to work as hard as the mind in meeting that challenge. It brings out only the adventuresome, the thrill-seekers who will face the danger, and have fun doing it. The Iroquois people have often been at the forefront to seek adventure.

At one time the men were hunters, stalking the game far from home. Then, they became warriors, travelling hundreds of miles to fight their enemies, both Indian and white, with legendary ferocity. They were also statesmen, conducting international relations and visiting foreign lands to defend the rights of their people in equally legendary oratory. The Iroquois were also explorers across North America as well.

There is a special excitement that comes from the challenge of each of these tasks, and no one but those who face them can appreciate that feeling. So, too, does Ironwork give an opportunity to overcome the odds, and succeed. But let's take a brief look at the history of Iroquoian adventurers.

The founding of the Iroquois Confederacy was a great adventure in itself, creating the image of the cultural hero—the Peacemaker. He faces all kinds of adversity and danger and still accomplishes a great deed. The oral history of the Iroquois is full of stories of facing danger, challenging the unknown, and with hard work, a good mind, and a little luck, the young heroes are successful. This creates a positive, and somewhat aggressive image of leaders, warriors and heroes for the Iroquois.

In 1710, four Woodland Indian chiefs travelled overseas to England to meet with Queen Anne. They described their own mission as follows:

"We have undertaken a long and tedious voyage, which none of predecessors could ever be prevail'd upon to undertake. The motive that induc'd us, was, that we

Richard Hill   129

might see our Great Queen, and relate to her those things we thought absolutely necessary for the Good of her, and us her Allies, on the other side of the Great water."

Imagine what those men must have felt, visiting a strange land, facing a foreign culture, unusual costumes, and becoming a media spectacle during their visit. They faced the challenge and survived the adventure. The gifts that they received overseas are still part of the Iroquois patrimony and stand as evidence of their mission.

In the 1790's several hundred Iroquois men, mostly Mohawk, were employed by the North West Company to secure furs for the company. The Iroquois were given the freedom to come and go as they pleased, to conduct far-ranging expeditions in new territories. By 1797, some Iroquois had made their way as far west as Prince Albert, Saskatchewan. These Iroquois fur traders had to cope with a new environment; they even had to learn how to hunt buffalo! They also had to face the hostile actions of the western tribes who generally disliked the Iroquois fur intruders. In one encounter, 25 Iroquois trappers were killed by opposing Indians.

By 1801, over 300 Iroquois had travelled to the Saskatchewan River area, and some made it all the way to British Columbia, discovering two important passes in the Rockies—the Yellowhead and the Athabasca.

Iroquois men had also become noted as voyageurs, and were often referred to as Canada's best canoemen of the colonial era. Mohawks had led the French troops under Denonville in the 1684 attack on the Senecas of central New York. Mohawk scouts also helped lead General Custer to his demise at the Little Big Horn. The Iroquois served as guides in the first arctic expedition of John Franklin, as well as the rescue expedition of James Anderson.

The point to be made here is that the Iroquois have a tradition of seeking adventure all across Canada, and that Ironwork can be seen as an extension of that need to seek adventure.

Introduction To Ironwork

The first of the Woodland Indians to become Iron-workers were the Mohawk of Kahnawake (Caughnawaga) on the outskirts of Montreal. In 1850 the Grand Trunk Railway decided to build an iron bridge from Montreal to Kahnawake. In exchange for permission to build on the Mohawk lands, the Railway agreed to hire Mohawk men as labourers on the bridge. That decision was to have a dramatic impact on the lifestyle of the reserve by introducing the Mohawk to bridge building.

Up until that time the Mohawk were noted for their skill as boatmen who could master the tricky waters of the Lacine Rapids. The Mohawks earned a living as quarriers, providing stone for Canada's emerging construction boom. Rail lines had come to Kahnawake and the Mohawk men would ferry passengers back and forth to Montreal. When the railway bridge was being built, the Mohawks first supplied the stone for the large piers to support the steel bridge.

At first the Mohawk worked on the old Victoria Bridge by both delivering stone for the piers and moving timbers and iron on the deck. The work of the bridgemen apparantly fascinated the Mohawks. The Mohawk labourers would wander out on the narrow beams and observe the work of the riveters.

Tom Diabo, whose grandfather worked on that Victoria Bridge, provided historian David Blanchard with the following recollection of how the Mohawks got into Ironwork, known as bridgework at that time:

> Back in those days us Indians used to work on the river, delivering big ships over the rapids to Montreal and Kingston. Well, when they was building the Victoria Bridge, not the one there now, the old one, men from town (Kahnawake) got work delivering stone from the quarry over behind "Blind Lady's Hill" to the masons on the bridge site.
>
> You know how Mohawks love to build things. So when the men from town were watching the bridge being built, some of the younger guys just climbed right up to take a closer look at how it was being done. The French men they had working there was so scared that they had to

hold onto everything they could so they wouldn't fall off. That engineer wasn't getting anything done with so many scared Frenchmen working for him. Of course, the guys from town wasn't scared. They just walked along the supports looking the job over, and checking out how the job was done. The engineer saw this and wanted to hire the Indians, but there was a problem, cuz most the men only talked Indian. So he hired a whole crew of guys from town, with a foreman who could talk English and French and Indian. This is how we got into the construction trade.

Although there is some disagreement on what happened next, it is commonly thought by the Mohawk of today that the real start of Ironwork began at the construction of the 1886 C.P.R. bridge at Kahnawake, referred to as the "black bridge." Mohawks were again first hired as labourers on the job, but demonstrated great skill at walking the iron. Records of the Dominion Bridge Company explain how the Mohawks became Ironworkers:

> . . . We would employ these Indians as ordinary day laborers unloading materials. They were dissatisfied with this arrangement and would come out on the bridge itself every chance they got. It was quite impossible to keep them off. As the work progressed, it became apparent to all concerned that these Indians were very odd in that they did not have any fear of heights. If not watched, they would climb up into the spans and walk around up there as cool and collected as the toughest of our riveters . . .

"These Indians were agile as goats," wrote an official of the Dominion Bridge Company in the 1940's. "They would walk a narrow beam high up in the air with nothing below them but the river which is rough there and ugly to look down on," he continued, "and it wouldn't mean any more to them than walking on the solid ground. They seemed immune to the noise of the riveting, which goes right through you and is often enough in itself to make newcomers to construction feel sick and dizzy . . . "

"We decided it would be mutually advantageous to see

what these Indians can do, so we picked out some and gave them a little training, and it turned out that putting riveting tools in their hands was like putting ham with eggs," he concluded.

Joe Regis and Napoleon Rice were said to be the first Mohawks hired on the Canadian Pacific Bridge job as Ironworkers. One year later, there were more than 50 Mohawk men working on the Sault Ste. Marie Bridge in northern Michigan. The men quickly formed new gangs, and trained the younger members on the job. Riveting gangs were in high demand and Mohawks become masters at that skill. Death soon followed, as Joe Diabo became the first Mohawk to be killed as an Ironworker when he fell from the Sault Ste. Marie Bridge in 1888.

These early Ironworkers were very different from those of today. The men wore heavy overalls and no gloves. The foremen wore white shirts and derby hats. Many even wore ties on the job. Yet, during the 1890's the Ironworkers acquired a nasty reputation for their rowdy behavior. They were often looked down upon by the other trades. Known as "Cowboys of the Sky", 19th-century Ironworkers were known to live a hearty, albeit short life. The Mohawks had found their challenge in the modern era and have become a welcome addition to the hazardous profession.

The economic need for men to walk the iron was the company's overriding concern as Ironwork was the most dangerous job at that time and there was a high turnover due to accidents and death. Unions were not yet formed and safety regulations were non-existent. Ironworkers only made 22 to 25 cents an hour in 1885. Yet by 1890, Ironwork had the highest accident and mortality rate of the construction trades. It is unusual to find an Ironworker who had more than five years in the profession.

At the same time as Indians in Canada were becoming Ironworkers, trade unions were forming in the States. The life of the working man began to change. The first eight-hour work day was instituted in 1893. The first unions were formed along ethnic lines in Chicago (German, English, Bohemian) and New York (German, English, Jewish). The profession's first journal was the "Bridgeman's Magazine" published in 1901, and is still published today with the new name "The Ironworker". However, the work remained dangerous. In 1904 twelve per cent of the Ironworkers were killed on the job. The only consolation was the hourly pay had risen to $4.05. Over two thousand Ironworkers were killed on the job between 1900 and 1920.

H.B. Moyer describes the personality of those early Ironworkers in his "Up Aloft with Bridgemen":

> Only men of great strength and courage become sky-scraper men; putting their lives in daily danger as they did, they developed a psychology of recklessness and violence that people in less hazardous occupations may find difficulty understanding.

Moyer also defined the skills of the 19th-century Ironworker as well:

> . . . must possess cool, clear head, a faculty for meeting and overcoming adverse conditions of all kinds, the knack of thinking in time of emergency, and an endowment of the highest mechanical skill.

Many of these attributes and personalities have remained the same for today's Indian Ironworkers; in fact most of them find that the combination of physical and mental skills is what attracts them most to the work. At any rate, the Mohawks found themselves a job that was both economically fruitful and very adventurous. Ironwork allowed them to continue their tradition of building, of facing a challenge and of showing their pride. The Mohawk sense of freedom was enhanced by the nature of the Ironwork profession.

A Day in the Life of an Ironworker

Every job is different. Each building has its own problems, its own character. Each pusher has his own ways of getting the job done. And just about everyone has their own nickname, earned out of respect or some act of foolishness.

Every day on the job brings a new challenge to overcome. Sometimes the challenge is to find a job. Life as an Ironworker certainly is not boring.

Once you get a job, either by waiting at the Union Hall or, if you are lucky enough to work steady for the same company, your day starts early. You've got to be to work by 7 a.m. and it's at least a two hour drive from your home on the reserve. Breakfast is coffee on the run because your ride comes too soon. You're out the door, trying to put on your coat, without spilling your hot coffee, or dropping your belt.

Your two buddies are talking a mile a minute, and driving twice as fast down the highway. Your mind is not following all the car-room conversation about the mistakes that the new punk made yesterday. You're too busy thinking about the work that faces you on the iron. You remembered how windy it was yesterday, how the whole building shook in the wind. Boy, you sure hate that wind, you lean into it, then, suddenly, it's gone, and you're staring below. Your friends bring you to earth with some wise-crack about how that punk-kid reminds them of you.

The rest of your gang is already there when your car pulls up to the job site—a four story addition to a car plant. They sip their coffee and wonder out loud if you're late because you like to sleep late or your girl friend doesn't. You've been at this job for five weeks already, and if the wind holds off, you can top off the job in another week. But you'll have to pick up the pace and show these other guys how it's supposed to be done.

The crane starts up with a big, smokey roar. The raising gang straps on their belts, the pusher shouts out some last minute commands, and the punk runs around trying to look busy. Up you go, first by ladder to the second floor, then up the column to the top. "Hey punk!," you holler like your'e mad. "Get me some three inch bolts, 3/4 inch . . . three inch I said . . . don't screw up this time punk." Off he goes like a midnight cockroach when you turn on the light in an out-of-town motel.

You sit there waiting for your partner to get in place, and it gives you a moment to survey the other workers, and their progress. On the floor below you is the bolting up gang, tightening the connection together. Those guys are mostly older, slower, and some say wiser Ironworkers. But you have to work on top for some reason, like your brother did, like your father did, like all the good Ironworkers did. You ask the bolting up gang if you should slow down so they will look faster. Someone answers with a comment about your mother.

There is nothing like early morning on the job site, the air is cool, the steel glistens, and the men are eager to get to work, even the ones that stayed out too late last night. They figure that the quicker that they get to work, the quicker they feel like themselves again, or at least the quicker the day will be over. The whole site comes alive and stays that way until 4:30 when you all hit the road for home.

The crane engine revs up with each lift of steel, as if you can hear how heavy it is. The air compressors sound louder than your cousin's hot rod, the one without the muffler. The impact wrenches hammer away on the bolts, turning the nuts, shaking the whole floor. The columns had to be plumbed up straight yesterday, but the "yo-yo's" make so much noise that you would think the steel might fall down. In fact, the piece that you just connected is only held by one small, temporary bolt, and now you have to walk out on that beam. But, you really can't worry about it.

Anyways, the day has just begun, you've got to hurry it up and finish the job so you can move on. In fact you have to hurry up the corner column because they are already sending the next beam up and your partner suggests that you retire. You look like a long legged racoon as you climb the column to make your way to the top, just in time to grab your end of the beam, guided from below by a long rope tag line. Your foot rests on a small tab of steel on the column. Usually you have to make a perch by sticking your pointed spud wrench in a empty bolt hole in the column.

First you have to remove the tag line and drop it safely. Actually, it is up to the men below not to work underneath you. They have to make sure to watch out for a dropped bolt, a flying rope, or even a dropped piece of iron. At any rate, you have to signal the crane operator with hand signals. A miscommunication at this point could cause you to lose a finger, or maybe, your partner's life. You have to trust each other, you have to trust the crane operator. This guy is really good, he pays attention, and he can move those big pieces of steel right into place, just like most people park a car.

You have to steady yourself, hold the beam and guide it in place, you signal for the operator to lower the piece, slowly, slowly, a little more, there, you have to slip your other spud wrench into one of the connecting holes. Check to see that your partner is making his point. Then you have to grab a bolt from your bolt bag and connect the two pieces together. Quickly you hand-tighten the nut, pull out your wrench, and then you realize that you made your point first, so you'll have to walk out on the beam to cut loose the steel choker. Soon as your partner is done you're on your way to the middle of the beam, walking gingerly but quickly. You signal the crane to lower the boom enough to slack off the strain so you can unwrap the choker. Down goes the choker, up goes the hook of the crane, and off you go to the next connection.

So there you are, not thinking of the wind, not thinking about anything except what you are doing. The old timers told you that concentration is everything to an Ironworker. Think about what you are doing, plan ahead, don't look down!

"Hey punk!," you holler again, "Where's my damn bolts? . . . How do you expect me to put this thing together without bolts, come on boy, get moving!"

Connectors are supposed to connect and move to the next piece, swiftly and efficiently. This time you don't have to move, but your partner has to slide down the column and go kitty-corner to the next point to be made. As he does, the guy who is shaking out the steel, setting the members in order, according to the blueprint, already has the next beam hooked on. From where you sit you can see the whole process, the iron on the ground, the crane, the men bolting up, the labourers making concrete forms, the pusher with the blueprints in his hand, the punk kid running for your bolts that you don't really need, the shanty where your lunch is waiting for you, the big tool box, the compressors, everything. You feel like you're in charge, you are on top. The only thing you can't see is your home.

But here comes the next piece and the whole thing starts over again and again, up to fifty times a day. The same steps, but the pace picks up, the pusher pushes harder, the steel sets quicker, and you slowly grow tired. Then, something goes wrong. A piece doesn't fit, no matter what you do. You have to check the number painted on the beam. It's right. But it's still wrong. You got to get a 16 lb. slidge hammer to kick that stubborn beam over. Bang. Bang. It shakes your teeth. Bang. Bang. It's hard not to get mad. Finally it's in place, but the holes don't line up. The bolt won't fit. You pull a drift pin from your bolt bag and hammer it in a bolt hole. Bang. Bang. The steel shakes and rings with each hit. Bang. Bang. Your arm is getting tired, but you have to hang on. Finally the holes line up and in goes a bolt. You leave the pin for the bolting up gang to deal with. Another floor takes shape, just in time for lunch. Even the steel seems to come to rest.

Lunch brings forth an appetite for food and stories. Laughter roars from the shanty with each story. A good dose of exaggeration makes any story palatable. Even the new kid relaxes a bit, but he seems to be avoiding you. The half hour always passes too fast. For dessert, a few quick instructions from the pusher, a handful of fresh bolts, and a mean look at the punk, just to remind him that he's a punk. Your unofficial job is to give him a hard time, to test him, to teach him. After all, you had to go through hell when you were breaking in. So now you get to find out what this new kid is made from, and have some fun at his expense. Some day he will appreciate all this harassment.

Afternoon. The day begins to drag. The steel doesn't shine the way it did in the morning. The sun is too hot. The wind doesn't help either. But the pieces keep coming, and you keep moving, and the building keeps changing. You can see just what you accomplished that day. You did better than you expected. The building is testimony to your day's effort.

Tomorrow will find you back on top, working until the job is complete. Another day, another job well done. 4:30

finds you packing your belt in the trunk, ready to hit the concrete trail home. As your car pulls off the site, you lean out the window and shout one last time, "Hey punk, not bad, now don't forget my bolts for tomorrow." It is the first time you see him smile. Tomorrow you will set even more pieces. You'll show these guys what Ironworking is all about. Just wait until tomorrow.

Tom Huff

WORKS: Four books in a limited edition of four. *The Sun Shines, The Grass Grows*, 1974; *Gustango Green*, 1976; *From One Owl To Another*, 1980; *We Do Not Always Walk in Beauty, We Stagger Down Sidewalks, too . . .*, (Six-writing color xerox), 1984; In Progress: *Nuclear Indians*, (essays on art) 1982.

THE SANTA FE YEARS: *Spearhead Press*, IAIA 1978, Co-editor, Weekly newsletter; *Corn Soup (And Other Good Indians To Eat)*, Editor, IAIA Literary Journal, 1979; *Red Earth Writers*, Chairman, IAIA Writers Group 1978–79, Public Readings, Performances, *Corn Soup*.

In addition to writing, Tom is an accomplished stone sculptor whose works range from large contemporary sculpture to Iroquois and moundbuilder stone pipes.

A Strange Relationship

When carving stone
The stone looks at me, as if to taunt
Carve me up, Tom Huff, carve me up
Smash me with your hammer and chisel
So I proceed to carve into it until
In a fit of passion, Hit a crack
And smash it into a million pieces
Now uncarvable, I sweep up the pieces
And throw them outside on the ground
As I walk away,
I hear the stones laughing.

I saw them
The little people
The other night
Deep in the Woods
Above Cattaraugus Creek

Around a fire
They were dancing the Dance
Which began all dances

The people were so small
Yet their presence
Brought daylight into the night

There were faces of old
Full of wisdoms which cannot be told
But that which is lived
The old ones smiled and sang to me
The young ones ran about, hiding and laughing
I was seeing legend come to life

I left some tobacco
And offered my hand in Reverence
They looked at me trustingly
They smiled and nodded
The dancing continued

I awoke at sunrise.
The tobacco was gone.

Homeland

Upstream Cattaraugus Creek
Along the ageless walls
Homes of the little people
Straight towering cliffs
Hold hidden secrets on every level
Legends of life
A place to think.

Downstream Cattaraugus Creek
Place of the Burning Springs
Roots of Ancient Villages
Where witches live they say
Legends of Gold and deer
A place to be

Gustango in midstream
Sloping green valley
Meets sheer cliffs
Two stone skips across creek
Small town of two colors
Garden gossip and peace
A steel bridge spans nearby
Connecting earth
And people
A place to live

Cattaraugus Creek
Flowing throughout
The common lifeblood
Of home and sacred places
Continuing cycles of life
Fishing   Water   Forest   Hunting
Legends of serpents and eagles
And Human beings
A place to respect

Turtlevision

Just as my Grandfather had said
It was during a rainy season
When the Great Cloud Turtle
Came over the mountains from the North
To cleanse itself once again

Remembering old legends
I waited and watched as it approached
A massive head peered out
Of an ever-expanding shell
Overshadowing the entire countryside
It floated slowly and evenly
As it neared me
The sky growing darker

As my Grandfather had said
It was the Spirit Turtle
Purifying its earthen body below
The shell of the Great Snapping Turtle
Which held up the earth and its original beings.

As the cloud passed directly over me
The rain stopped and the winds ceased.
Looking up into the mist, as if in a dream
I saw my Grandmother breaking unwanted pots
And burying the shards in the mud
The Turtle lowered its head
Gazing down at me with lightning eyes
Then its huge tail
Cast a last shadow on me.

Two days later, I heard that Three Mile Island
Was destroyed by a mysterious storm cloud.
I smiled.
Just as my Grandfather had said.

Alex Jacobs/ Karoniaktatie

Bios are funny things, like padding resumes when you need to, or even when you don't, like poofing it off to appear nonchalant and successful. And the photos! Like grainy snapshots of the Loch Ness monster or clear images of a good-looking vital artist. But when they eventually meet you, you're a wee bit burned out round the edges. Gee, he used to look so good. Well, usually I would say use the images from my work as that's what I will look like by the time anyone who reads these books gets around to actually seeing me. It'll be like "you're just like I expected." And if you can't find images of yourself in your work, then why are you doing it?

My work can be found in Native poetry & literature anthologies (*Come To Power, The Next World, The Remembered Earth, The Clouds Threw This Lights, Songs from this Earth on Turtle's Back*), magazines like *Contact/II*. Co-editor, co-founder of AKWEKON (along with Peter Blue Cloud and Rokwaho) that had a great run, but as a magazine is resting. AKWEKON as an idea and project still lives. What about an AKWEKON music publishing/record-tape label or a gallery or a mobile media gallery or anything that's urgent or dynamic or practical or necessary?

You may find my sculptures and paintings or ceramics and prints in galleries. (I've been doing horizon /river/ stripes/landscape icons and on the road/ crossing /converging/ contrary mementos-in-motion. The sculptures tend to be non-precious/ non-important items/ materials made precious or important. You know, the commercial vs. the real.)

Been working as a DJ/programmer for CKON FM, totally owned, operated and licensed by the Mohawk Nation Council. Been known as LXJ and DOC and I think those names are gonna stick. I've been trying to get to Santa Fe or "back to Santa Fe," as the saying/feeling goes and I think this time I'm gonna make it. But I'd like to be on the road, on the move, bringing AKWEKON on the road, starting and joining other AKWEKONS all over the country/landscape.

So, see you in Santa Fe . . . or one day up north here in the mountains or on the river.

The Politics of Primitivism

Concerns & Attitudes in Indian Art

Indian Art, what is it? may be the biggest question of all. There can be complex answers as to culture, history; there may be simple answers as to economics. They can further be reversed in that culture can explain things in intent and attitude simpler, but when we talk of contemporary Indian Art in the marketplace, we get into complex attitudes of commercialism, presentation and colonization or acculturation. Culture separates but also brings Native People together (there are enough clues and common references to initiate any exchange); economics are similar most everywhere in the arts but the differences can be quite divisive, intense and contrary.

We talked of crafts and art, craftsmanship and artistic attitudes; as well as the society that looks upon this and makes the differentiations between art and craft. One of my art teachers in critiquing a sculpture student's piece, told him to check out the laborers downtown working on cement. Those guys take their trowels and in steady, trained moves, they make the student's work look . . . well, bad. No matter how artistic or conceptual the piece is supposed to be, the details detract from the whole piece. There are many sides to this argument, but the kicker was in the critique the teacher kept pressuring the student on his 'concept' and principles or objectives. When the student gave in somewhat on his artistic stance (after being baited by the teacher's best hatchet critiquer), the teacher made his point by saying, 'Well you sure gave up on your principles quick'.

So artists need to stand for something, against many odds; they need to incorporate craftsmanship in their art, their creativity, to 'clear the path' toward their objective. So, is the 'common' laborer also an artist or craftsman? From my own laborer experience artistic types don't exactly fit in to some scenarios, they tell you just to Do It, 'You're not painting the Sistine Chapel,' and move on, doing the best you can. To be the best, of course takes practice and training, just as art or any other endeavor. Would you go further to say that laborers find a place within them to bring their actions and minds together, yet also can be somewhere else thinking about home, afterwork, etc, sort of like Zen Construction? They are not seduced by their materials or objectives, they observe and are part of a flow, the objective being, don't mess up, be consistent.

In society, as we know it, they come up with tags like 'common laborer', 'artist', 'craftsman', and will place people by their place in society, their class, position. So, are we industrial workers, devoid of faces, just hands and muscle; or management types with overloaded brain compartments to do specific jobs, and let others worry about their jobs and even the meanings of consequences of 'jobs'. And what about those busy art 'workers' who are classified as true artisans by their society, brought together on the level they call CULTURE. Somehow, those that make and those that buy or patronize are lifted up from the common masses, and into a high society, or the top levels of a hierarchal culture. So, where does the Native writer or artist fit into this? Or do we?

Acculturation is a Two-Way Street

This is so obvious that most people, educated or not, miss it. Acculturation and assimilation can go both ways and there are endless examples as to Our Cultures (native, folk, indigenous, tribal) acculturating the 'civilized' into free-thinking, democratic individualists, wary of a central authority that prescribes certain attitudes, etiquette and laws **downward** to the masses. Conformity is the issue; in Indian Country, under Indian Law, we all have the Right To Be Different. While our lifestyles were romanticized (by both non-native and later native writers/artists) and elements were taken from Our Culture into Their Culture, it is also obvious that the **intangibles** were not taken in with the gifts or elements. Each element had a relationship to all things, so many connections came together in one piece of everyday life. NOW, when that piece of culture that-once-was is displayed as Art, artifact, relic, object . . . where are the connections, the relationships? Their culture is all about this categorization, documentation, scientific analysis, a separation of all elements into a **reconstruction,** or to us, *a re-creation,* of the Creation itself . . . which is of course profane, the Creation being All Sacred in its entirety and in its elements. That is where the connections are.

To an over-educated 'skin like myself, the intangibles are not seen, but they are there like fibers of primal light which we have long since forgotten how to employ. But to the cultural resource person, traditional or contemporary, it is not intangible; they will describe exactly the functions, the relationships, the actions and reactions of Natural Physics . . . the ripples in the pool of life.

Art Is Meaningless

I once tried to explain this theory, but it didn't work out too good. What I meant was, ART, as it is known in the dominant society (the acculturated sponge called civilization) can mean nothing when we talk of Art in the Indian perception. As They have taken from us, leaving behind the sacred and taking only the material, they end up with profane, mundane objects or relics. They can imagine and re-create the ritual of creation or everyday life that manifested itself into an object, a utensil, a keeper of memory . . . but it is only imagination and theory, guesswork. And they are paid handsomely to theorize all day long.

When 'skins walk into the ghostly museums, they feel more than they can see . . . the artifacts are so lonesome, so devoid of human contact, they almost cry out to be touched and used, to be taken away back To The People . . . back home. They are ghosts, spirits, tied to the past with those fibers of light. We are the connection to the future, the unborn, with these artifacts, spirit-objects. But Museums are all about Law, separation termed preservation, hierarchy called Culture, etiquette that separates classes of people from their common heritage while attempting to SHOW us that we were all related at one time, but that is the past. By severing the past, we are forced to confront present existence as the only way, the only reality, the only possible existence. They seek to legitimize our present civilized course by educating us to the Past as untouchable, unknowable. The good ones, with good intentions, do realize the potential of the human past as tens of thousands years of experience lay before us, waiting for people to make connections, understand the relationship and the ingenious hands and minds and carefully crafted memories through which the teachings of Creation flowed.

So this shows that something now termed Art does mean something to us, something totally meaningful even sacred. But ART, as we know it now, can miss this . . . can be so educated and inbred as to be blind and callous and arrogant; just as the so-called culture of society or civilization plainly operates in its business-as-usual circus. The visionary artists of the recent modern era knew this on their own terms. They reacted against the norms and values of the day to create the best of what is called ART. They freely took from Native Indigenous Cultures, sometimes it was acknowledged, many times it appears as pure thievery. They call this 'influence', 'eclectic', 'affinity', we can call it 'plagiarism' and cultural thuggery as well. Cultural thuggery is my term for Cultural Colonialism of the most paternalistic, chauvinistic kind. They actually take, never give back, never acknowledge in respect, and proceed to call it their own, and visionary genius as well.

Indian Artists must make connections between grassroots people and traditionals, as well as contemporary culture and presentation/commercial values. So Indian Art that has no reference points, no commonality, no roots, no language, no connections to the past AND future, can be meaningless. Why else does it hang in pawn-shops, or called tourist art, McDonald's Art, Bank Art, Mall Art, why else is it churned out in studios and sold for instant gratification by an artist who needs to survive, and accepted in equal gratification by the buyer who needs to have an Indian on their wall, or buy into Americana, if not to assuage some of their collective guilt. This may seem bitter, but the potential that goes unnoticed and the talent that is utterly disrespected by the mainstream or establishment is where this bitterness is directed.

Art means something to us, but when we seek to transfer values from the sacred to the profane . . . we act just as they do in their blind assimilation of The Things That Are Ours into things that are now theirs. We can not assimilate these ways, we must reject them, alter them, adapt. The transference or transmutation of **values** lays at the heart of problems in Indian Country. And Indian Country is an affectionate term for the whole Earth . . . the Land . . . Mother Earth . . . Father Sky . . . the Four Grandfather Winds . . . the Grandmother Moon and her seeds that give us life. To forget or ignore basic Indian values, traditional values, human values, Natural Law . . . is a crime. And crime is what High Society and Cultural Thuggery and Expanding Civilization are all about. To the highest offices in the Land will reach the best criminal minds. The wealth of the Earth will be controlled by the best organized criminal gangs. The values of home, community, tradition, spirituality will be transferred into jobs, jobs and more jobs disconnected from Reality and Human-ness.

We must not act as cannibals to our own culture. We must not act as they do; we must not sell what is not ours to even give away. Sharing, though, sharing is a word, a value, that is full of meaning. In Art, we must share our visions, we must investigate these values. The positive nature of acculturation is **sharing**, the negative is cannibalization or greed. Our lives, our Culture, our children's heritage depends on us; the Earth depends on us . . . or will purify herself of the poison and the poison-makers.

Who Knows Turtle's Song?

who knows him?
who took us from the slime
who carried us upon his back
ugly & cold & hungry
they call this creature
he is all that is dark: past, present, future
it is he that crawls in the back of your head
"remember   where you come from   who you are
no matter what you will become and discard
on your journey from dark to light
remember"

cold in his mundane calculations
    he survives
brutal in his constant hunger
    he endures
ugly in his beauty
    he never changes
he has no memory, no duty
    these he leaves for you
only this is his: a heartbeat that knows full well
    each season and shift

Turtle sings (yet doesn't know why)
a humming longing sighing song
that lasts full moon to new moon
as he gazes and blinks, quietly trilling,
he scratches in the sand the same path over and over

While you light your path and in doing so
find other paths and you need a changing of the guard
just to keep track of your candles
he will never leave your mind, you must kill him

to cover your escape, to become something else
there is no way to change without erasing his memory

so you scrape out his meat
leaving behind an empty shell
that rattles in the dark
humming and singing songs
it doesn't know why

Joined the Nation

i ain't seen him in awhile
yeah, he joined the nation, he did
& i wonder, where i been?

join the nation & you leave behind
the dopers & potheads
the hard core drinkers
& social drinkers with their
vigilante ways & business buddies
& the laws etched in stone
of Who is Right & Who is Better.

its not being better or being right
its being old & new at the same time
its being hard like the old-timers
& trusting in people to also
work & work hard
You leave behind the easy ways
the easy money with the invisible
fingers with every bundle of cash

building better mouse-traps doesn't solve
the problems (i told the Indian poet
living in NYC), it just leaves more bodies
of bigger mice, more often

you have to measure the wholeness
and day to day decisions are made too easy
by people who do not care for the future
only their present

& i'm glad he went over to join the nation
& i know he can see & feel the full measure

& where i been? in some strange wilderness
of money, cars, gas, rent, schools that put out
the best cogs for the biggest machines
that make day to day decisions
while you sit & watch TV

why is it the best, biggest, most efficient
can not measure the full measure
& use food as a weapon
to beat the hungry senseless
& use communication to make people
confused, complacent & envious

in a world of passivity & entertainment
this brother instead joined the nation
& strengthened it, he made a decision
& doesn't want to be entertained by
the media circus, he already knows the
ending to that story

Movement

WE SAID: This is us, all of us (akwekon), not just we
    but you
Never left, never gone, always been here, always will
we said: stand up, don't believe all that's handed you
on government green communiques
listen to them that have something to say
not them eager to talk with papers & maps &
    directions
looking at their watches & 20 year plans
demonstrating with clean graphics their deed & title
from divine right/manifest destiny/imminent domain

Listen to the learned, the tattooed & the scarred
not the Know-it-all, mr & ms Clean, the actors, the
    front men or their right hand hatchets
Listen to the questions, not the answers

they said: Not us   never here
we got free elections & sometimes people vote
we pay taxes, we pay people good to mind our
    business
turn off the news, get Happy Days
i thought someones solved those problems long ago

now it's you, saying us & them   we told you so
but you wouldn't listen   first us then you
that's the way it goes   not right or wrong, just late

now, there's an undercurrent across this land
in the nodding grain raising its collective head
in the purple mountains shouting defiant "Don't Touch
    Us"
in the cities where Seattle & his ghosts walk

along with frozen urban spirits who refuse to leave
not knowing they are spirits
no one ever told them how to be spirits

these mystic warriors signal a return to fight
in my belly one ties a hunger knot
wait, wait, he says, not much longer

they told me 10 years ago, it will happen in 10 years or
    so
i listened, but i forgot, caught up am i us or them

but movement   it never stops

Paul Rosado, 1982

Maurice Kenny

Born and raised in northern New York near the St. Lawrence River and the foot-hills of the Adirondacks, Maurice Kenny currently lives in Saranac Lake, N.Y. An Associate Professor, he is Writer-in-Residence at North County Community College. Mr. Kenny has authored numerous collections of poems, including *Blackrobe* (1982) which was nominated for the Pulitzer and was recipient of a National

Public Radio Award for Broadcasting, and *The Mama Poems* which received the prestigious American Book Award in 1984. His work appears in many important anthologies: *From the Belly of the Shark, From the Hudson to the World, On Turtle's Back, The Remembered Earth, Songs From This Earth On Turtle's Back, Earth Power Coming, Words in the Blood,* and *Harper's Anthology of 20th Century Native American Poetry.* Joseph Bruchac has written that Mr. Kenny is . . . "achieving recognition as a major figure among American writers. Already seen by some critics as one of the four or five most significant Native American poets . . . a distinctive voice, one shaped by the rhythms of Mohawk life and speech, yet one which defines and moves beyond cultural boundaries." Michael Castro, author of *Interpreting the Indian,* has also written, "His work is American Indian, personal and universal all at once. His work is characterized by both historical and spiritual depth." Mr. Kenny's most current collections are: *Between Two Rivers* and *Humors And/Or Not So Humorous.*

Listening for the Elders

is summer this bear
  home this tamarack
are these wild berries song
is this hill
  where my grandmother sleeps
  this river where
  my father fishes
does this winter-house
  light its window for me
  burn oak for my chill
does this woman sing my pain
does this drum beat
  sounding waters
or does this crow caw
does this hickory nut fall
  this corn ripen
  this field yellow
  this prayer-feather hang
  this mother worry
  this ghost walk
does this fire glow
  this bat swoop
  this night fall
does this star shine
  over mountains
  for this cousin who has
  no aunt picking sweetgrass
  for a pillow

is summer this wolf
  this elm leaf
  this pipe smoke

is summer this turtle
    home this sumac
    home this black-ash
is summer this story
is summer home
is twilight home
is summer this tongue
    home this cedar
    these snakes in my hair

reflections on this sky
    this summer day
    this bear

Going Home

The book lay unread in my lap
snow gathered at the window
from Brooklyn it was a long ride
the Greyhound followed the plow
from Syracuse to Watertown
to country cheese and maples
tired rivers and closed paper mills
home to gossipy aunts . . .
their dandelions and pregnant cats . . .
home to cedars and fields of boulders
cold graves under willow and pine
home from Brooklyn to the reservation
that was not home
to songs I could not sing
to dances I could not dance
from Brooklyn bars and ghetto rats
to steaming horses stomping frozen earth
barns and privies lost in blizzards
home to a Nation, Mohawk
to faces I did not know
and hands which did not recognize me
to names and doors
my father shut

Legacy

my face is grass
    color of April rain;
arms, legs are the limbs
    of birch, cedar;
my thoughts are winds
    which blow;
pictures in my mind
    are the climb uphill
    to dream in the sun;
    hawk feathers, and quills
    of porcupine running
    the edge of the stream
    which reflects stories
    of my many mornings
    and the dark faces of night
    mingled with victories
    of dawn and tomorrow;
corn of the fields and squash . . .
    the daughters of my mother
    who collect honey
    and all the fruits;
meadow and sky are the end of my day
    the stretch of my night
    yet the birth of my dust;
my wind is the breath of a fawn
    the cry of the cub
    the trot of the wolf
    whose print covers
    the tracks of my feet;
my word, my word,
    loaned
legacy, the obligation I hand

to the blood of my flesh
the sinew of the loins
to hold to the sun
and the moon
which direct the river
that carries my song
and the beat of the drum
to the fires of the village
which endures.

Passions

From: Tekonwatonti: Molly Brant

Yes, oh yes . . . passions for blackberry
blossoms, the clank of deer bones winning games,
river water sluicing against canoes,
snow covering old plum trees,
smells of horse sweat after a fast gallop,
sounds of mice scratching, the touch of cat fur
against thighs, good black coffee with sugar.
I have a passion for hot bread and salty butter
sweating its brine. I have passions . . . how
they misuse this word, sensation . . . I have passions
for baby gurgles, giggles, sour currants, honey,
moose meat, fried corn mush with maple syrup,
Willie rubbing my back. All sorts of things:
green woods, black rivers, red birds, corn soup
steaming late winter afternoons when dark falls
and Willie is hungry from cold fields.

Solely, they think my passions are anger.
They accused me of demanding his head, and that
I kicked it across the parlor floor my black eyes
flashing as the blood stained the rug and wall
where it came to rest; the tight mouth and weak
chin, open grey eyes bulging in tornado storm . . .
scared and frightened of this child's wrath.
They'll say anything to destroy my happiness.

I loathe war and blood; I think continuously
of spring, wind rustling in green corn,
violets ripening at the wood's edge,
young possums sucking life into their jaws.
I was taught to keep love in my heart,
honor my leaders, bring wood to the fire,
respect the smallest insect and the furthest
mountain. I have urged men to paint and ready

for battle; I have definitely . . . I won't lie . . .
teased, prodded, ridiculed warriors to defend the
    village,
and I did cry for blood of the French. No one
heard my wails at the death of my uncle, Hendricks,
as his bones rotted in the woods near Lake George . . .
never to return to our village for burial.
I hate war, but love this earth and my kin more
than I hate battles and bravery. This
is my passion . . . to survive and all around me.
This is why I mount my raven gelding
and cry out at dawn to the young warriors
to throw off the robes, put their morning
pleasures away, send their women to pack jerky
for a long march to defend our priceless
right to new dawns and darkness, the right
to old songs. I lead an army . . . yes, me, a girl
    . . . painted like a man, and I would thrust
a lance into all enemies' hearts and rejoice
at my enemy's death and our victory. Who would not
defend their mother's womb. All around me
is my mother's womb. I lay claim to it.
This is my passion . . . life and the right to it.
Which includes those blackberry blossoms,
the marsh iris, the growl of bear, the light
rising and falling upon the roofs of our lodges,
the rivers that bathe us clean and slack our thirst,
and the old plum tree flowering winter in snow.

Moving the Village

From: Tekonwatpati: Molly Brant

Runner:

Crow has called ten times:

River waters are empty. The sun
does not show salmon. The creek
gags on the bones of trout.
Your corn grows smaller each summer.
Soon it will be stunted from under-nourished
soil and kernels look like ragged teeth
in the mouths of dried old witches.

You will starve. You have not re-placed the soil.
Nor have you allowed the doe to feed her young;
bear complains there is no honey in the hive,
birds are angry there are no cherries.
All you have are holes at the wood's edge
that stink from your feasting.

The seekers say to dismantle your house;
fill baskets with your accoutrements, utensils,
drums and turtle rattles,
carry the old and lead the young.
The seekers have found a village where the pine
grows tall in unfettered air and rivers run fresh.
Hawk soars high above berry vines and corn
will grow, and squash. Wolf is fat.

Thank the sun for rising on this place of many birds.
Leave tobacco on the rocks. Look up and down
and all around you; then follow and be strong:
think of the mountains north from here.
Remember the bones you leave behind
and the spirits who need meal.

The seekers advise you to march under stars,
greet dawn within the new circle.
A fire waits your pots.

Yaikni

I

Lena heard their laughter as she watched the other women picking berries in a distant patch. She lazed in the morning sun, content to watch the women and stare at the sky busy with birds cutting clouds and decorating trees. Overhead, a crow flew south, cawing shrillingly to the workers in the field.

"*Agaya, agaya!*" she whispered to herself. "*Agaya!* Dog! Ol' crow, you're like a dog, wandering from back porch to porch sniffin' for dry bones." She waved the crow away with a stiff hand.

The meadow, covered in chicory blue and hawk weed orange, sloped from a wooden knoll down to a rushing creek bordered by iris and skunk cabbage. A short walk from the village, the meadow had been picked clean every spring for as many years as the oldest villager could remember. Late June, directly after summer solstice, the berries were always there, usually in profusion. And the women always came to pick even though they cultivated hybrid berries in gardens behind the barns. No larger than a thumb-nail, they were always delicious, sweet as rich honey, red as the setting sun. Spring's first gift. Children, of course, usually ate more than they dropped into the berry cans slung on their little arms.

Lena now recalled the many times she had walked to this patch with her own mother. How much she actually disliked bending, stooping, kneeling under the broiling sun to pick hour after hour. Once she had a nose-bleed, and her mother led her into the shade of a beech tree, dressed the injured nose and allowed her to play the rest of the day with a doll. She learned fast – to pinch her nose. When it bled, her mother would invariably take her out of the field. Since the first bleeding she could not eat berries. The very thought made her blood run. But there she was now, after all those many, many years picking berries with her daughter and her own great-granddaughter. After many years away from her home village, kin, the patch. She wondered if her nose would bleed now, again. Well, she wouldn't pick too many. Wouldn't bleed. She'd just sit quietly, pluck one or two for her own tongue, perhaps tease little Annie with one, and ignore the empty bucket beside her in the grasses.

"*Agaya.*" She called again after the crow now only a fly-speck on the sky.

The sun slowly moved south in no hurry, rising higher and higher. The near-cloudless sky shimmered in heat vapors. The trees on the woody knoll sent long fingery shadows down across the meadow. Lena's glance followed their trail up the knoll. She knew the cool, the shade of the maple and the birch, the elm and sumac, the scotch pine. She ached to find a tall sycamore and sit under it, her back leaning against its comforting bark. Scanning the woods on the rim of the knoll, she spotted an old man leaning on a cane. His back bent in age. His hat brim covered his face. She thought it shrouded his face. Of course, it was Mr. Peters. *Onkiakenro.* An old childhood friend. Still breathing, alive, like herself, wandering like the crow, a dog, from house to house, sometimes offering cheer, sometimes a salve for a burnt finger, a remedy for a cold or common-sense advice. He'd visited her twice recently. Came to her daughter's house right to the supper table, sat down, drank tea, and hardly with a "thank you, mam" strolled out into the night's darkness. He'd barely said a word. She remembered how he'd been such a quiet boy. Now he was a silent man. Mr. Peters vanished into the woods.

"Gramma, I wanna go home. I wanna go home, Gramma. I'm tired."

Annie was fretting.

Children had no real appreciation of work, of berries, of being in an open meadow, of the warmth of the sun. Wait until their bones are old and dry, the hollow sockets whistling with wind, break at the touch of a breeze. No appreciation at all. Why do they bring the little ones anyway? Always tired, always thirsty, never want to relieve themselves in the bushes. Always hungry. And they ate more berries than they put in the bucket. If the men want jam and shortcake, then they should keep the children with them. That wouldn't do, surely. The women'd go home and find their little arms broken, eyes put out, little bodies burnt. Men were not good babysitters for sure. Useless to argue. Foolish.

Again she heard the women laughing. A good story probably or some rare gossip.

Sluggishly, lethargically she plucked one little berry not much larger than the end-knob of her thumb. Very red, very juicy, and she dropped it into her bucket with six others. She just didn't feel much like picking today. She was tired too. Like Annie, and thirsty. Could eat a cookie if she'd thought to have brought one. "Oh! Boy!" she exclaimed aloud, "good thing I went before we left the house. I'd be in a fine fix."

A mosquito flitted around her wrinkled face, and she shot out a hand to grasp it but failed the mark. It landed on her ear-lobe and stabbed. "Monster." She drew away her palm and a spot of blood glowed on the sweaty flesh.

"You alright, Ma," her daughter, Lulu, called out.

She nodded. "Yes," she called back. "Mosquitoes." She forced a big smile so Lulu could see she was doing fine, but under her breath she whispered, "*Agaya.*"

She rolled seven little berries around in the bucket with her stiff fingers. One-two, three-four, five-six, seven. Seven little berries. Seven little dwarfs. Seven little gifts from the Little-People. She felt good, real good, thinking of the stories of the Little-People her own mother had told in the berry meadows. Of how they gave the strawberries to the ragged boy who had in turn given them his hunt, squirrels, to eat when they were starving. How they protected still to this moment the people from the forest witches. She chuckled. They were good stories. Good stories. The Little-People are good people. She plucked a berry which was slightly larger than the usual. It still had a white bottom, like a baby's bottom. She shrugged and patted the whitened bottom tenderly and dropped it pell mell into the bucket. It was hard. It rolled around like a boy's marble.

Again wisps of laughter came from the other women squatting in the blue meadow. Gossip, the source of all stories, she thought. Oh! if it were only winter and they could sit in the parlor and tell stories, forget this heat, this back-breaking work. Have coffee and Lulu's shortbread cookies. And gossip of the old days, times. But there weren't many left from the old days. Not many. A few. And she'd forgotten most of them, the stories and the old friends and relatives. Been away tooooo long. Too long.

She held up her hands. "Dog bones," she whispered. "Bones. I'm all bones."

True, she was thin, not an extra ounce anywhere on her body. Lulu said she'd fatten her up. Corn soup would do it. Mush. But all she really ever wanted to eat was pop corn. Lulu laughed at this at first. And then a frown replaced the laughter. Then a scowl, finally a brief scolding. She didn't gain the weight. And she was glad about that. She was just naturally skinny though her six sisters had been heavy to just plain fat, obese. She knew that had killed them all, one by one. Fat. She abhorred fatness. Just like those gossiping women over there in the field. They were all fat. Great rolls of it hung from their arms and thighs. They'd live to regret their greed, their fat.

Not far off she heard Annie squeal. "Gramma, a mouse. A mouse, Gramma."

"It won't hurt you."

Above flew a hawk, but she knew it would not descend for its lunch, not with those laughing women making so much noise. She felt a little sorry for Annie who'd been surprised and she felt sorry for the eventually doomed mouse. And she, indeed, felt sorry for the hawk who would do without food. Well, it was probably too fat anyway. No, not really, hawks and other creatures knew better. They knew how to survive. People had gone silly gobbling down all the food they could push into their mouths and stomachs. Downright silly.

As she predicted, the hawk flew off to a branch of a dying tamarack at the eastern edge of the meadow. It took a stance as though ready to defend the territory of its hunt, waiting for the women to abandon the field to make its kill. Lena could feel its eyes burn into her back.

One more berry plopped into her bucket. Child's play, she thought. This is child's play. And as though competing with her great-grand-daughter, she commenced to furiously pluck handfuls of berries and tossed them into the bucket. The fruit was overripe, squashy, so glutted with juice the sticky waters ran between her knobby fingers curled with arthritic curves. She flung the mashed berries to the others and reached down for more, her gnarled hands touching down into the sun-warm vines, the crisp leaves turning red like the fruit itself, like paint, like phlox, hibiscus . . . wild flowers, like blood, menstrual blood, hospital blood, scarlet like the morning star, crimson like clouds afire at sunset, red like the spanked bottom of a naughty child, like anger on the cheek. Chagrined with herself, her own present laziness, apathy, her sense of competition with little Annie finally took hold and for moments she busied herself with work, bending under the noon sun and plucking berry after berry, refusing to taste even one, to slip undetected one sweet berry between her teeth. Shortly, the bucket bottom was covered. She took a breather, languishing from work in the heat.

A soft breeze brought a bug into her bucket, a lady-bug fell into her fruit.

"Lady-bug, Lady-bug, fly away home. Your house is on fire and your children are alone. Lady-bug. Lady-bug, fly away home. Lady-bug, Lady-bug, your house is on fire, your children alone. Lady, Lady. Lady, Lady-bug . . . "

She couldn't remember the entire rhyme. She chanted over and over, "Lady-bug, Lady-bug," hoping the rest of the words would follow. She worked herself into an anger so vicious she began pounding the air with her fists. Clenched hammers, the rolled hands struck the air, and the vines, the ground, her own chest.

"Ma! Ma, you alright?"

The women picking further away now in the wide meadow looked up from work.

"Ma, answer me. You alright?"

Her eyes looked up from the vines. They were seared with anger. Her glance turned toward the knoll. There he was again lurking about the woods. Mr. Peters. He stood in silence like a tree framed in a windless mirage.

"Ma, answer me! You alright?"

Lulu's voice grew, concerned, louder as it came closer.

"Lady-bug, Lady-bug. Fly, fly, damn you, fly away

home. Or I'll burn down your house. I'll cut off your children's heads. Damn you."

She picked up the bucket and flung out the berries.

Lulu stood by her mother and motioned to the other women to hurry. She looked at the old woman among the berries, her faded blue house dress soiled with scarlet juice, her hands and face running red, her bunned white hair framing the startled face was flecked with berry stain. She pulled out the comb that kept her hair in place and it cascaded down like the rapids of a swift river.

"She's a *witch!*" Annie screamed.

"Get out, get out," the old woman cried.

"Gramma, she's a *witch*, a witch!" little Annie screamed and screamed again as she stomped her feet.

"Get out of my bucket and go care for your children! Out of my woods. Out of my way. My house is burning and my children are alone."

Annie began to dance in a circle around her great-grandmother crying and, terrified, tearing at her own dark hair. She screamed and pushed her hands against her face and eyes to hide. She thrashed about, breaking from Lulu's inept grasp, and ran off to the women hurrying towards Lulu.

"Get out of my bucket. Out! *Agaya, agaya.* You filthy dog! Leave my bones alone. My bones are mine. Scat, I say, scat. You fell in my berries. Get home to your children, get home!"

The sounds, the words came from the very center of her total being, her long years of hurt and disappointment, frustration and her loneness in a world she then could not possibly comprehend. Her madness, these insane actions bubbled from her blood, the sinews of her flesh and spirit, a spirit half broken by life itself.

"It won't go home, Lulu. It won't go home, Lu. Its house is burning." She wept. Hot tears streamed from her eyes red now with pain.

"Mama, Mama, it will go home. It will, Mama. It'll go home and protect its children."

Soothing, but Lulu's words could not possibly penetrate.

She threw her hands to her tear-stained face and hid behind the bones. When she pulled them off her brow,

her cheeks, her chin were smeared with red juice. It trick-
led in jagged rivulets down the withering flesh of her
throat.

"It won't go *home*, Lulu."

"Yes, it will, Ma. Everything goes home, Mama.
Everything."

"That damn lazy Lady-bug won't."

"Ma, quiet down."

"I'll put her house on fire."

Lulu hugged her mother close. They weaved like a mul-
lein stalk wobbling in the faint breeze brushing the
meadow.

"What's wrong? What happened? Lena, you alright?"
the women questioned.

"I don't know," Lulu responded. "I just don't know
what happened. She's screaming about a lady-bug and
pointing to the hill."

The older woman cried wretched tears. She slobbered
like a child.

"The sun's gotten to her, Lu. Better take her home. Let
her rest."

Lena simply stood, her reddened hands immobile at
her side, her dress stained with sprinkles of berry juice,
her face smeared and contorted, her frizzled white hair
lifting gently in the breeze. She stood like an admonished
child, guilty and shamed. Her back stooped, she was broken before the women, before her grand-child.

"Annie, come now. We're going to take Gramma
home."

The child had run off to a thicket of crabapple and
knelt behind the sapling bushes crying for Lulu to come
fetch her away from the witch. The witch who would
chop off her head, burn down her house, and suck out her
breath — just like in the stories Lulu has told her winter
nights ago.

II

A bat darted in and out of maple shadows
above Mina Mount's head. She walked quickly down the

twilight highway. Her back was killing her from stooping most of the day at berry picking, and the sun had caused a brute pain to pound at her temples. At that moment, she'd prefer sitting on the couch watching "The Joker's Wild" on TV, but she was out of bread. None for supper and none for her husband's breakfast. The road was brightly lit by a flashing red and blue neon sign and one gas pumplight. A car was parked by the pump, but as she approached the driveway it roared its motor and pulled away into the darkness of the night.

Mina opened the door. A bell tinkled overhead.

"Just a loaf of bread, Hattie. That's all I need."

"You been berry pickin', huh?"

She heaved a sigh and replied a low, "Yes."

"I see the sun on your nose. Fiery red."

"We picked 'til about three. Ol' Lena Bottoms gave out."

"Gave out?"

"Had some kind of fit. Said she couldn't get lady-bugs out of her bucket. Started hollerin' blue blazes. Poor Lulu. Couldn't do a thing with her mother. Just held on to her close. Little Annie ran away. Screaming her grandma was a witch. She did look it with juice all over her face. We took her home to bed. I don't envy Lu. She's got her hands full with that ol' lady, I'll tell you."

"Lu should never have brought her back up here."

"It's her home, Hattie. She was born here."

"Yes, she was born here, I don't care. She didn't ever much live around though."

The shopkeeper took the dollar bill offered.

"She lived down there in Brooklyn all those years with that Irish guy. You know, I can't remember her living here, can you?"

"Not really." Hattie handed out the change from the bill. "Well no, I can't remember her, only the stories, and they were wild and thick."

"Gossip."

"Maybe. I don't know. Lu's about my age, 'bout fifty. Lena left when Lu was five, six years old. I know Lena's sister, Mary, brought her up."

"Right, she sure did."

"Lena drove down with some Caugnawaga men from

Montreal who were going to work in steel. Never heard from her again." She slammed the cash register shut.

"Not directly, Hattie. Heard *about* her."

"Yeah. Those men came back with some high tales. She was fast. Hittin' all the bars. Kept a lot of boys happy, they said."

"Right. *They* said. Probably gossip. I recall my mother saying Lena had a rough time when her Tom died. Guess there was a lotta love between those two."

"Maybe. Why you suppose Lu went to Brooklyn for her?"

"She was bad. No money, no man. Was in some kind of house getting sick." She pointed to her head and twirled her finger in the air. "Batty. Lu isn't the kind who'd let her own mother die in a place like that. Even that Lena had abandoned her. Lu's a good woman. Hasn't been easy on her all these years either. All those boys she had to raise after her own man died."

"Funny how he went hunting and never came back from the woods."

"Some hunter probably shot him for deer and left him to rot. Well, she's just got the one boy and Annie left. He'll never go now his own wife ran off. Suppose Lu thought her mother'd make good company."

"Suppose. Get a lotta berries?"

"Plenty. Gonna jam some, freeze some, and eat some tonight. Okay. Gotta get back for supper."

"Night!"

"Night," Mina called out and shut the screen door behind her.

III

Though it was late they were still at the table eating supper. Lulu cut a pork chop into little pieces for Annie who sulked in her chair, straining to avoid contact with her great-grandmother who stirred tea in a pot.

"Eat it up now." Lulu pushed the plate before the young girl. "Ma? More potatoes?"

Before Lena could reply, a knock was heard at the door

which opened by itself. Mr. Peters stood within the threshold. He walked into the kitchen without bidding a good evening or an apology for obviously disturbing the meal. That was not like him at all. Mr. Peters never entered a house without invitation. Lulu was perplexed by his actions.

"Have a chair, Mr. Peters."

He commanded a chair next to Lena. "*Onkiakenro,*" he said, glancing at his old childhood friend. "*Etsagnon!*" Lena didn't understand. She'd been forgetting her language.

"Feast?" Lulu asked the guest.

"*Etsagnon,*" he repeated. "*Akoserakeh*-winter."

Lulu was perplexed. She didn't know what to say, how to respond.

Lena avoided his face, the lines which had crept into the brown skin now darker from the new sun. She poured tea into her cup, blew against the liquid, and then poured some into her saucer and sipped.

"*Akoserakeh,*" he said again in a low voice.

"Been a hot day. We've been berry picking most of it." Lulu made some attempt to sociability even though she knew he wasn't listening to her. Instead, he took a pipe from his pocket, a pouch, filled with tobacco, lit it, drew a gulp of hot smoke and exhaled. Lulu urged Annie to eat her chop.

"Ma had a touch of sun. She's doing fine now."

Lena spilled tea on the tablecloth.

"Look what Gramma did."

"Hush. Gramma isn't feeling good."

Mr. Peters drew more smoke and blew a small puff to the right, another to the left, one puff was blown up and another was blown down.

"*Etsagnon,*" he said quietly.

"I don't understand." Lulu was not only perplexed but now nervous. Why a feast. And then, that moment, right now? When then?

His voice was dark as his flesh, deep and rich though gentle, soft as down. Though spoken quietly, the sounds filled the kitchen. His eyes danced and his black hair fell across his brow, making him appear a much younger man though he was certainly Lena's age. There was a black prominent mole to the side of his right eye and it drew Lulu's attention.

"Sure you won't . . . " She stopped from asking if he wouldn't take some tea. It wasn't the time. He hadn't come to socialize.

Lena grew fluttery, jittery. She rose from the table, excused herself, and wandered into the parlor.

"Ma's not been well since she came home."

The man nodded agreement.

"The move, the trip north, settling in, well, it's been hard on her."

"*Akoserakeh*-winter. It won't be long before snow will cover the fields."

He spoke to the air of the room, the corners of the poorly lighted kitchen, the dark windows glazed from the single light bulb hanging above the table.

"It'll stay long, this time."

Lulu was not only startled but now thoroughly upset. Had he gone batty too, like her mother.

"Dandelions are withering. The pretty weeds."

He pinched tobacco from his pouch and blew a sprinkle onto Lena's vacant chair. "Already the seeds fly on the morning breeze."

"Yes. Spring came fast, and summer goes fast. Corn is knee high in July. Got squash on the vines." She almost gurgled out words. "My beans aren't doing well." She rattled a forced conversation but received no appropriate response from Mr. Peters.

He took from his shirt pocket a small feather and placed it on the table.

"Blue-bird, blue-jay."

Lulu's nerves were decidedly on edge.

From another pocket – he seemed full of pockets – he drew out a pinch of soil, earth dark and rich, so rich it appeared a melon could sprout from its womb, the tiny mound that it was.

"Sweetgrass on the air."

"We've got to start cutting for baskets soon."

"Sweetgrass on the air," he repeated as though to remind himself, his remark not necessarily meant for Lulu. "I'll go." He stood, went to the parlor door, touched the wood frame and returned to the table. Glancing down

180

at little Annie who sat frozen in fear, he again reached into a pocket and withdrew a small Kraft jam jar, unscrewed the lid, stuck his finger into the contents, sucked his finger dry, screwed the lid once more into place, and set it down upon the white tablecloth.

Lulu was quiet. She knew. In her own aging bones she knew. Yes, she knew. *Etsagnon.* Outside, off in the distance she could hear men singing. Their voices raised on the early summer night, dark and heavy, solemn and penetrating, constant.

Mr. Peters stepped to the door, rattled the knob and walked into the night.

She stared at the jam jar. Just stared, hardly breathing. She stood and circled the table. Annie had stayed absolutely quiet. Now she broke into tears. "I'm tired. I wanna go to bed, Gramma."

The singing stopped. The sound of a drum crossed the night, but only momentarily. Then the drum stopped too. Was silent.

"Can I go to bed?" That was strange coming from Annie who fought every night the eventual need to go to her bed.

"Yes, your father will be home soon. Yes, go to bed."

Annie commenced beating the cut up chop she hadn't eaten with her fork.

Lulu knew. Yes, she knew. Everyone knew but Lena, her mother. Maybe Lena did know. Maybe. She got Annie washed up for the night, into pajamas, and tucked under cool sheets. She strolled listlessly back into the kitchen where she cleared the table and washed the dishes at the sink. When that was finished and the dishes put up into the cupboard, she went to the parlor.

Her mother slept. Short staccato snores thumped the darkness. Lulu turned on a light, went to her mother's rocker, bent and kissed her on the cheek. "Oh," she exclaimed benignly, startled by her rash action. "I haven't kissed my mother's cheek since I was five years old. Not since she went away. Not since she . . . left me." She stared down on the sleeping old woman withering away into age, withering into greyness, whiteness. Her cheek and brow were as white as the tablecloth. She'd been out in the sun all morning and not a drop of color.

This paleness wasn't natural. She spotted a blotch of red berry juice stuck hard in the old woman's white hair. "We missed some, Mama, when we washed you up." She smiled and left the parlor.

In the kitchen again she remembered the Kraft jam jar and picked it up. Slowly, hesitantly she unscrewed the lid. "*Yaikni.*" She raised the jar to her dry lips. "*Yaikni.*" She swallowed the strawberry juice.

Lena's snores ceased. She was deep into dreams.

"*Yaikni,*" Lulu repeated, and screwed the lid in place.

The night was quiet except for a fire-bug beating against the kitchen window. "*Yaikni,*" she breathed the word again, and again, "*Yaikni.*"

She slid into a chair and buried her face in the apron still bound around her waist.

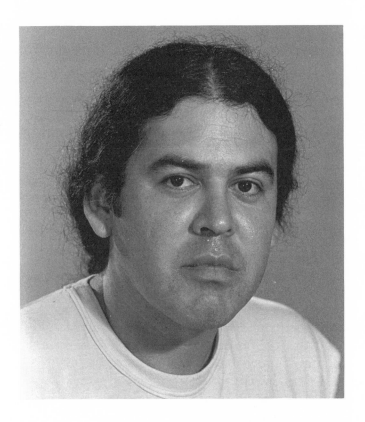

Bruce King

Writing, I tend to think, should be an expression of emotion, ration-alization flamed by passion, a symbolic, literary hunger released and spent on the pages for the enjoyment of the reader. A scratching, typing, bleeping art form that keeps its inventor's imagination work-ing and grasping until the wee hours of the night. Personally, I draw on everything I've ever known. People, places, happenings, hopes dreams, confrontations and defeats. Art, like life, is not always pleas-ant and beautiful, at the same time it is not always seething and ugly. More often it is a mix of both. Writing just sorts it all out through the working of the inner eye. The eye that sees the gruesome, brutal murder take place before a spectacular sunset merely by written sug-gestion. Native people have always had a knack for art regardless of its manifestations. The richness of our backgrounds, traditional or contemporary, is riveting, not only to non-Natives, but to us as well. The only distinction we should have to make is whether it's good or bad and that embodies everything.

At one time she could take your breath away
from way across the room
merely by dancing dark eyes in your direction
a tilt of the head, a shift of the shoulders
and all the cowboys could care less
if it be an intention or a disregard
as long as the trail led to a place
to lay their heads on her shoulder
in a dark hour of passion lit
by the burning end of Marlboro country

So they used and abused her while her youth
drained away, till it filled and satisfied
the conjured images, themselves, in the saddle
with sweet talk like spurs, a riggin the same
the object of the hard ride, competition
till she lay spent and broken
and given to the fear
like the horses they rode
at the all Indian rodeos

When she became everybody's, and nobody's
she stepped into her own needs to fulfill
in the darkness she found the heartbreaking vacancy
that giggled and laughed in her sleep
and followed her through the honky-tonks
while it held her on the dance floor
and lit up her cigarettes
placed a hand on her knee
and a blurred tear in her eye
like so many cowboys
singing the blues

184

So she washed the sorrow down
with a shot of Black Jack, and told her story
over and over and over again
while her regulars whispered
and lied about listening
and rubbed up against her in her pain
while the story went on
all the way to the cars
and the galas that followed
they may cry when they finish
but they laugh when they're rolling

That night she rode with death thinking
why not, I've been with everyone else on this
god damn reservation
when the ride was over
and left her somewhere in the next day
she smiled, cause death
had his
and left her like the rest
stained and alone

When the north wind blows in across
a sick and angry Lake Erie, in the gray
dismal yawnings of early winter
withdrawing trees turn their backs
and splash themselves in shades of blood

The sun will peek behind the cold
and dreary blankets cling to life
in fifty two shades of frost and mist
when summer jumps to winter
in disregarded passion, leaves behind a weeping
     autumn

Your head bent for the onslaught
you cover your eyes in anticipated hibernation
and reach for me with gnarled, broken hands
left over from a summer of lust
for everyone but yours truly

Still I take stock in your whispers
and check into my winter resort
an unheated room at the local heartbreak hotel
blanketed on a stool in a creeping draft
I'll manage another winter while you heal

A Contemporary Chant to the Great Spirit in the Genre of Modern Attitudes and Epoch

Oh Great Spirit, are you really there? If you're listening as I hope you are, we approach you with open hearts and bloodless hands, seeking your everknowing knowledge and wisdom. Once again, we humble and meek people beings have gone and stepped into the eternal big deep. Have we been abandoned, or did you just dim the light that once guided us? As our voices echo through the time tunnel we wonder how that shining, guiding force has moved to the end and left us stumbling around in the darkness, or have we done the unthinkable and started walking backwards . . . no, we're too bright these days. Or maybe it wasn't you at all. Maybe all the fluorocarbons we've been blasting into the air for the past fifty years have had an adverse effect on the shining of your light? Wouldn't that eat away the protecting shield and let more light shine through? Then the ultra violet rays would have to deal with the toxic chemicals that float through the air of this world you've created. No telling what kind of chemical combustion and gases we might achieve from that, but not to worry, there's always acid rain to shower the whole bursting, smeltering mess down upon the four-leggeds and two-leggeds. This is really deep, Great Spirit. You see what I mean about needing your wisdom. I mean, this is, well . . . like this is your creation you know, you have to tell us what to do. I knew you were going to say you told us all of this a long time ago, but you can't expect us to remember everything, right? I mean, we got things to do too. You know Great Spirit, this is all the white man's fault. That's right, if it wasn't for him, we wouldn't have the pollution problems we're having. What's that, oh, you mean my Mercedes, . . . hey, it's got the latest catalytic converter money can buy and I only use it to go back and forth to work. Work. To make money. Down at the steel plant . . . the place where the spillings are dumped into the river. But hey, that ain't my fault. White men started doing that long before I was born. Besides, it's all wrecked now and You can't cry over spilled milk. Anyways, what can I do? Stop? Hey, I can't stop . . . I got kids to feed, a mortgage to pay off, who's gonna pay off my insurance? Hey, I know, you're the Great Spirit and all, but there's a real world out here baby and if you don't get into the dog eat dogism, you get left hanging in the wind. Get my drift there buddy? Yeah, I know there was once a way to treat one another, but no one does things like that anymore. No, not even the real people, and that's the white man's fault too. He introduced capitalism, corporate structure and materialism. It ain't so bad if you learn the hustling process. Cost? There ain't no cost. It's all gain. It's how you're to play the game. Brotherhood? Man Great Spirit, you just don't get it do you? Okay, listen, if you're going to kick butt, expect to get a little poop on your shoes, aye? Am I right or what? The land? Well, we got a little bit left. We're taking real good care of that. Tribute, what kind of tribute . . . oh that. The old duffers take care of that stuff, besides, I don't know nothing about that stuff. Time? Well, I hang out at the bowling alley, at the bar, watch TV, and hey . . . I just got a new VCR. I don't have to blow a lot of money taking everyone to the movies anymore, heh heh, see what I mean about getting over? Thankful? Of course I'm thankful. I exercise my rights as an Indian. I buy my cigarettes from the rez, my gas too, cause I know I'm helping out Indians. I think it's great that we got bingo now. Man there's more bread on the rez than there's ever been. You know what I heard . . . I heard there's slot machines popping up and ole Uncle Sam can't do nothing about it. Ha! I love it! I'm thankful for all of that and I've been thinking about investing a little savings of my own into a bingo hall back on my own rez and, hey . . . could you give me a hint on how my future looks, with me sticking my neck out on this bingo trip . . . I figure you'd be the guy to ask. No? It's alright, I understand. You know it really is good talking to you Great Spirit. The old geezers back home said it would be. They say, whenever your mind is unclear and you're burdened with despair, impart your thoughts to the Great Spirit and he will receive them. You know it works. I feel much better already. Well, I figure I've taken enough of your time and I got a date tonight . . . don't worry, heh, I keep discreet and she doesn't even suspect. But, I'll stay in touch Great Spirit, we'll do lunch. . . .

William T. Laughing / Atonwa

I am 40 years old and live on the St. Regis Mohawk reserve. I have held many different kinds of jobs from Director of an Indian Center to teaching to laborer. I once held a job as a flagman on a paving crew which inspired "Em'ty Sea." A man from the em'ty sea was the man from the Ministry of Transporation and Commerce. MTC was on his car and all his equipment. A joint is where two halves of pavement meet and must be rolled when fresh and the new pavement is black as midnight. The stardust is the shiny white tape that marks the temporary lines on the road.

Currently I am looking for work and carve cradleboards on the side.

© wtl Atonwa 1977

Em'ty Sea

I was walking down the line,
My sign in hand,
And waving passers down with my free hand,
Behind the man rolling his joint,
Behind the man putting his midnight down,
    putting his midnight down.

The man from the em'ty sea,
A roll of stardust in hand,
Said to me, "Lay a strip every so far."

I was walking down the line,
A roll of stardust in hand,
With my sign in my other hand,
And waving passers down with my free hand,
Behind the man rolling his joint,
Behind the man putting his midnight down,
    putting his midnight down.

Dead fox on the side.
The money's good,
If you don't get clipped.

I was walking down the line,
My two hands lay a strip every so far,
A roll of stardust in hand,
My sign in my other hand,
And waving passers down with my free hand,
Behind the man rolling his joint,
Behind the man putting his midnight down,
    putting his midnight down.

I went to the man from the em'ty sea.
"Here's your roll of stardust."
Said I, "It's em'ty, see?"
"I don't have enough hands"
"For this job for two,"
"What extra is for me?"

"Son," said he, "you'll get nothing extra"
"From me, but an em'ty check"
"And a roll of stardust"
"That's not em'ty, see?"

I went walking down the line,
My two hands lay a crooked strip every so far,
A roll of stardust in hand,
My sign in my other hand,
And waving the passers down with my free hand,
Behind the man rolling his joint,
Behind the man putting his midnight down,
        putting his midnight down.

Peace Maker

Long before columbus,
Lost and hungry,
There was the Confederacy
And before then,
There was De-ye-no-da-donh,
A virgin life-giver.

A baby she bore,
No man the father
Disaster and ruin would come,
So to the ice covered water
Went the family
To drown the babe.
Three nights did they try.
And three mornings was he found
By his mothers side.
He was accepted then,
For great was the path
He must walk.

With love he did grow.
Beauty surrounded him
With a glow from his spirit.
Strong and handsome was he,
De-ka-na-wi-dah — named by a dream,
And none other would be so named.
Jealous of his nature,
His people abused him
And cast him out.

South did De-ka-na-wi-dah strike,
To the land of the Mohawks
To whom he greeted,

"I have come to give you help."
"Come," they said.
"Share our council and our homes."

He saw, day by day,
Life lost by wrong deed or word.
Danger even to fetch water.
He called the people together.
"The maker of us all,
"Never meant for us to kill one another.
"Our lives were meant to be full,
"In peace and safety.
"Love, not hate,
"Should be shared
"By all the Creator's people.
"The Maker of all led me to you
"To bring about a great plan of peace.
"Peace will be yours and your brother nations
"You will war with brothers no more."

The Mohawks considered his words.
"There is truth in what you say,
"But a test is needed.
"We will kill you.
"If you return,
"Then we will know
"That this law of peace,
"You will find."

De-ka-na-wi-dah responded
"This I can do;
"But the manner of my death
"Will be of my choosing.
"I will climb the tallest tree
"Above the waterfalls
"Cut the tree
"And I will fall
"With the tree and the waters."

This they did.
The next morning,
At breakfast,
Alive and uninjured,
They found him.

Later,
He met A-yonh-wha-thah.
Together, they went
To the Mohawks,
To the Onieda,
To the Onondaga,
To the Cayuga,
And to the Seneca
With the great plan of peace.

The brother nations together
Uprooted the tallest pine from Onondaga;
Threw in their weapons of war;
And replanted the tree
As a symbol of their brotherhood
And the new confederacy,
Long before Columbus,
Lost and Hungry.

Red Blue and Red Gray

Yoh-Nah-Wey Yoh-Nah A Wey
Creator, why do we battle?
Tribesmen fall with thunder.

Yoh-Nah-Weh Yoh-Nah-Weh
Creator, this is not my war,
Yet, here we wage on a gray army.

Yoh-Nah-Wey Yoh-Nah-Weh
Creator, aid us in this battle,
Let not my people fall.

Nee-Ee-Ti-Tah-Tah-Tah
From where comes this other chant?
From the other side!

Nee-Ee-Ti-Tah-Tah-Tah
Are these brothers we fight?
They too cry for the Creator.

Yoh-Nah-Wey Yoh-Nah-Wey

A storm comes up — so dark,
Yet, still we senselessly fire.

Yoh-Nah-Wey / Nee-Ti-Tah
What is this buckskinned giant
That now stands over the field?

Nee-Ti-Tah / Yoh-Nah-Wey
All keep firing — yet none are hit.
Creator, is that you?

Yoh-Nah-Wey / Nee-Ti-Tah

Morning—He is gone.
We meet our gray brothers on the field.

Nee-Ti-Tah / Yoh-Nah-Wey
Our shells spent, in a mound,
Where he stood.

Yoh-Nah-Wey / Nee-Ti-Tah
The Creator made us red.
As Brothers we again stand.

The Great Mother's Lament

My people have been with me a long time.
They came to me.
They sat on my lap,
And we spoke with meaning.
We learned to live together.
They became my children.
When they were hungry,
I fed them.
They took no more than needed.
They wasted not. We shared.
We became plentiful.

A short time ago,
Another people came to me.
They ignored me and called me a thing.
They took more than needed,
And left the rest to rot.
They pulled my hair,
Never to grow again.
They destroyed and changed my children.
They poisoned me and my life streams.
Yet still they take.
Soon, I shall give no more.

Richard Hill

Oren Lyons
(Jo ag quis ho)

A faithkeeper of the Turtle Clan of the Onondaga Nation, Oren Lyons was born in 1930 in Syracuse, N.Y. Chairman of American Studies at SUNY at Buffalo, he is an author and has illustrated publications. He is the publisher of *Daybreak*, a quarterly national newspaper devoted to Native American views. He has been an active leader in the social and political awareness movement among the Iroquois Six Nations. He has also worked on other Native American concerns through participation in programs sponsored by international organizations such as UNESCO, the International Council of Indigenous People, and the Russell Tribunal. He resides on the Onondaga Indian Nation, Nedrow, N.Y. where he is a member of the Onondaga Council of Chiefs.

Power of the Good Mind

"At some time in the future, you will see the chief of trees, the Great Maple, begin dying from the top down. At that time it will be a warning to all that serious times are upon us, and to take heed to our conduct. . . . " Thus spoke Handsome Lake, Seneca chief and prophet of the Haudenosaunee, as he delivered the "Gaiwiio" or "Good Word" in 1799.

There was a front page story in the International Herald Tribune in Zurich, August 8, 1987 that made me think of the words of Handsome Lake. The story was titled "When the Alps Changed—Sudden Italian Disaster Raise Questions of Humanity's Relationship with Nature." This caught my attention because it was the first time I had seen a news story recognize a relationship that Indian people take for granted—our relationship with the Earth, our mother.

The story went on to describe the floods and landslides in the Valtellini Valley that have killed 44 people since July 18th. "The high and mighty Alps of the Valtellini giants . . . seemed incapable of change," the article stated. "The mountains did change, and now they are dangerously fragile."

"We have to go around on our tip toes right now because they could crumble at any minute," stated an Italian geologist. According to some newspaper columnists and politicians, people have damaged nature in Valtellini by constructing over 30,000 vacation homes over the last 20 years, deforesting the mountain to do so.

To the north of Italy, the famous Black Forest is now suffering a blight that has the potential of killing the whole forest in our lifetime. The culprit is acid rain from the industries of Great Britain and Western Europe.

Here in North America, Canada and northern states

are complaining about acid rain falling on their territories from the industrial complexes of the Great Lakes.

The acid rain is killing fish life and fragile flora and fauna of the lakes, rivers, streams and ponds. The trees are dying and there is a growing alarm that if this destruction continues at its present rate we will witness irretrievable environmental loss in our lifetime.

Last spring, there was a statement from the Vermont Maple Sugar Association that the maple trees were dying from the top down. The Maple Growers Association was irate demanding something be done about the fast rate of deterioration of the Maple trees. There was a toxic chemical spill in the Rhine River recently attributed to human error that resulted in a fish and wildlife kill that will require years to repair. This spill originated in Switzerland, long known for its attention to natural resources.

How can we forget the Chernobyl disaster that contaminated a great portion of Europe? The reindeer herds were devastated and the radioactive contamination of the water and grazing lands threatened to wipe out the culture of the reindeer herding Sami of Sweden and Norway. The Soviet Union has not acknowledged its responsibility to these people.

DDT contamination has reached the fish and seals of the northern Pacific, and is following the great currents of the seas, carrying this contaminant to the four corners of the earth.

This is by now rather common knowledge. We know the sale of DDT is outlawed in the United States where this deadly chemical is produced. Why not stop the continued sale of DDT to Third World countries. If it is too toxic for America, shouldn't it be too toxic for others?

The point to be made here is obvious. Mankind is responsible for most of the destruction of the environment in the world. The world is an entity that lives, and with the great force of our Uncle the sun, produces the life that sustains all of us. Most of the world has been subjected to exploitation by human beings. Great herds of animals are now decimated. Many animals and birds are becoming extinct. Each year they are displaced by and for human beings.

As great populations of mankind grow with absolute disregard for local sustenance, the earth becomes depopulated of animals, birds, trees, shrubs and grasses to the detriment of the general quality of life. The fish life is fast becoming decimated and we are eating types of fish that our last generation considered trash. The so-called wildlife (natural world animals) – a misnomer that could be attached more accurately to the human being species – has had to adjust to the culture and communities of people.

I recently saw the body of a red fox in the downtown section of Syracuse, New York. In my mind's eye I pictured other dead animals I had seen along the highways – deer, raccoons, groundhogs, hawks, and varieties of birds. The sight of this fox was different. This sighting was near downtown. What was he doing there? Where was he coming from and where was he going? The fox, one of the wariest of animals, difficult to see in the forest, was here, downtown. A variety of questions came to me and as I mused about that unfortunate fox I could only surmise that it was hit by a car as he tried to cross the expressway.

Several nights later I was driving into the same city. As I passed a large cemetery near a hilly suburban development I saw three deer by the highway – two adult doe and a yearling. They hesitated as I slowed to stop, and instead of turning back to the safety of the woods beyond, they crossed the road in front of me and disappeared between the houses of the city. I knew there must be some fields beyond the houses. The question arose in my mind as I thought once again about the fox. Where are they going?

Maybe some of the people who lived there knew the deer came in the night, but I doubted very many were aware. For the animals it was dangerous, man's nature being what it is. Yet, the deer were going directly into a human community, upon their own volition. Why?

It is a question I cannot answer, but it is a manner of accommodation. It reminded me of my Indian people of the past. They too, went into the white-man's community, putting on his coat and tie, and attempting to accommodate to this strange society. The result was mixed. Some survived, most didn't.

Did the deer survive? Probably. I don't know. The fox didn't. Both were wearing their own coats. Their accommodation is one of survival. They carry knowledge and secrets of survival. How many more of the animals live with us without our knowledge – the coyote in Los Angeles, the hawks in New York City.

One thing is certain. They can only survive as long as we do. We are displacing them from their home daily. We are displacing the future generations that our Great Law says we must protect. In protecting them, we protect ourselves. The great spiritual law of peace says that all life is equal and a manifestation of the Creator's will. Therefore, we must respect each life as such, and recognize that we are journeyers who must depend upon one another. We must seek the spiritual values as our guide as we were all instructed at one time, we must take responsibility for our actions and activities.

We must see with the clarity of those animals that survive among us, wearing their same coats, and we must reciprocate their interaction. We must see with the vision of those that give us direction so long ago. They knew we would come to this. The message was in Handsome Lake's words," . . . Take heed to our conduct . . . " We must learn to use the power of the good mind. The end of this little discussion we will write by our own conduct.

Water is a Sacred Trust

"There will come a time when the good water that we use to cook our food, cook our medicines, and clean our bodies will not be fit to drink . . . and the waters will turn oily and burn . . . the cool waters that we use to refresh ourselves will warm and heat up . . . our misuse of this water will turn it against us and people will suffer and die . . . "
Handsome Lake, Seneca Prophet, 1799

Thus spoke Handsome Lake to the people, his words preserved among the Haudenosaunee or Six Nations Iroquois in the oral document that survives as the Gaiwiio (the Good Word). The message was given to the people through him that year, and has been repeated in Six Nations Longhouses annually to this time.

He spoke these words at a time when most of the streams and springs were still pure and his words challenged the imagination of Seneca people of 1799 to perceive such catastrophes. Today we no longer need our imagination to see this. We need only look about to see his vision. How much farther into the future did he see? In my opinion we are experiencing only the beginning of that vision, and the responsibility for the future of the coming generations is in our hands.

We must come to understand the natural law. The natural law holds that water is the first law of life and we humans share the need for this water equally with every form in life. Indeed, we are water. How have we arrived at this time in the history of the world with such a poor report on the condition of our life-sustaining support systems?

Is it ignorance? Or just careless neglect? Is it that there is no respect for water? No ethic but exploitation? Is it the fundamental belief that science will always find an answer to our excesses? Is it the growing industrialization of civilizations?

Yes, to all these reasons, and more. The past hundred years have been the most explosive in mankind's history – world population growth, technological developments, medical knowledge and breakthroughs, energy developments, space programs, nuclear power, industrial pollutions, world armament and the devastations from modern warfare.

Drought and pestilence are nothing new to mankind; toxic water is. Today most great rivers across the world are used as sewers; industrial and human waste are poured into these life-giving arteries daily in countless tons. Woe to those people downstream, and to the oceans themselves, the eventual receiver of all this pollution. What about life and the people downstream in time, our grandchildren and their progeny? It is they who will pay the consequences of today's exploitation and excesses.

The Sunday New York Times, December 6, 1987 ran a story datelined New Delhi by Sanjoy Nazarika:

"The Indian government reported that hundreds of people have died in areas severely affected by drought, and health authorities attribute most of the deaths to contaminated water and food . . . thousands of Indians die every year from waterborne diseases such as gastroenteritis, but the official statement indicated that the current drought, the worst in the century, and the shortage of drinking water in the seven states worst affected were being blamed for the latest deaths . . . A large number of deaths in these places is most likely to be attributed to bad drinking water because the people are drinking water from whatever source available . . . "

There is always a reason for what's happening to these life giving resources. If you ask the poor people who are always the ones most directly affected, they will say simply, "We have no choice; we must survive." If you ask the corporations or the people in control, they will say, "We have no choice. It is a matter of economics. We cannot afford the costs of reconstructing our plant to accommodate the waste." If you ask the government, they will say, "Yes, let us establish a committee to investigate the problem." Not much ever seems to change, and the sewage and waste continues to be dumped into the rivers.

What is lacking is leadership in government with the courage to challenge the corporations who are primarily responsible for much of the environmental pollution. Local, state and federal governments seem to lack the political will necessary to produce laws with force enough to make these corporations and companies comply with healthy regulations.

On the other hand, the companies and corporations need to change their present philosophy to comply with healthy environmental regulations and long term goals that make development, environment, and finite resources compatible to meet the burgeoning needs of the coming generations. Not an easy task, and some will tell you impossible. However, the alternatives are even more impossible.

The human race is going to have to change its values and goals. Somewhere along the way the societies and civilizations began to lose the old standards of responsibility for one's actions – to family, neighbors, and societies – gave way to a selfish 'me' society. Immature and insensitive to fellow man. The results have been an increasing gap between the haves and the have-nots, and an increasing loss of the sense of community. The family has suffered in our contemporary societies and the result has been an increasing loss of family ties and estrangement between parent and child, particularly with the teenagers. The young adult is less prepared to bring up a family because they have been denied the support of the grandparents, aunts, uncles, and cousins, and lack the lore of family life.

I apologize for generalizations, but these observations show a consistency that is disturbing. This has to do with the future well-being of life on this planet we call Mother Earth. Obviously if we do not prepare our children for mature responsibility, they and their children will suffer even more, and be even less prepared to meet the challenges of life in their coming days, which will have many times over the magnitude of our problems today.

Amidst all of this negativism, there are extraordinary things happening that signal leadership and responsibility to the future. Coalitions of nation states, organizations, groups and individuals are taking place. They are focusing on issues and generating the energy needed to attack these issues. More important, there is an international perspective to all of this – nationalistic borders are giving way to common interests, and that is what is necessary to achieve global solutions.

In October such a 3-day meeting took place in Denver, Colorado and moved to Estes Park in the Rocky Mountains for 5 more days of workshops and conclusions. The Fourth World Wilderness Congress, dedicated to conservation and positive use of our natural resources and wilderness, gathered for the first time in this hemisphere. Vance G. Martin, president of the sponsoring organization, The International Wilderness Leadership Foundation, sounded the theme, "It's a matter of human survival."

Conservationists gathered from around the world, representing 51 countries including China and the Soviet Union. For the first time, Indians from North America were invited to present our view of the natural world and contemporary societies. The Traditional Youth and Elders Circle participated. We presented three statements from the indigenous peoples' perspectives.

The first statement came from Norma Kassi (Wolf Clan) Vuntat Gwitch'in of old Crow, Yukon Territory, Canada. Her message was the indigenous peoples are the wilderness. If you destroy wilderness, you destroy them. She spoke of her people's laws, what they take, and what they give back, and she said, "there are no political boundaries for the caribou."

I delivered the second message on behalf of the Traditional Youth and Elders Circle. My message was about the natural law and that we are bound by the law of life regardless of what we are – the human race, the green life that grows, or the animal nations. We are all under the same law of the land, air, water, and spirit.

The third message was delivered by our grandfather elder, Magqubu Ntombela of Zululand, South Africa, and he said the same about the land and life and our responsibilities. He talked of the "White Rhino" and its powers and the need for the good minds to gather and council for the welfare of future life.

The inspiration for The First World Wilderness Congress was from Magqubu Ntombela the Zulu tracker, and his close friend and companion Ian Player, a white man from South Africa and an ardent conservationist. They work together on the Wilderness Leadership School, a concept that brings diverse people together to one campfire over a period of a week or more to share the fundamentals of life. It is a trek into the wilderness where the earth is the school and Magqubu and Player are the guides and teachers. Other people, including Indians, are starting similar projects, both in wilderness training and in practical homesteading. There is a lot to do.

Keynote speaker to this great congress was Prime

Minister of Norway, Mrs. Gro Harlem Brundtland. She presented a report that was prepared for the World Commission on Environment and Development of the United Nations addressed to the global community. The term "sustainable development" replaces "economic development," and productive management of environment and economy will insure adequate resources for future generations.

We were inspired to renewed efforts by Mrs. Brundtland's energy and dedication to the future. In my opinion it is fitting that a woman lead the way for future generations. The women have too long been exempted from the leadership decisions concerning life, considering the mess the male dominated world is in at this time. It is time that the natural law of male and female, equal partners in and for life, once again prevail. Perhaps, along that road at some point in the future we will again see and taste the power of pure water.

John Kahionhes Fadden

David McDonald

A Funny Thing Happened on My Way to Meatball Hill

Many Winters and Summers (not to mention Moons) ago, near the waters of the mighty St. Lawrence, upon the Mohawk land of Where-The-Partidge-Drums (Akwesasne), was born David "Bobcat" McDonald. The year of his birth was 1943 (his wife suggests it's more like 1902), and he is one of seven children raised by Mose and Mary McDonald. He attended local schools graduating from Salmon River Central in 1961, and began a career of dairy farming following in the foot-steps of his father. In 1965 Dave married Edith Adams (a very patient woman), also of Akwesasne, and they have two sons, Adrian, Jason, and a daughter, Sherry. Their home is near the farmhouse where Dave was born, which is a little east of "Meatball Hill," over-looking that part of Cook Road called "Spaghetti Corners."

Dave is the antithesis of the "stoic Indian." His dark eyes are a far-cry from the "stoney stare" of Hollywood's stereotypical Indian, and, instead, reflect the titilating twinkle of a humourous soul. A day, an afternoon, or even a half-hour with Dave is punctuated with gut-wrenching laughter as he relates a recently heard joke, or shares a "slightly" exaggerated anecdote. He has his serious moments, clearly necessary for the good son, husband, father and friend that he is . . . but, "life is too short to take it *all* too seriously." Thankfully, he doesn't, and those of us who know him are fortunate. He is a funny man, and during this serious time, facing Native People, of land claims, bingo halls, and political realities, it is refreshing to share his chuckling-view of the human experience.

LIFE ON THE FARM

The Beavers and Frogs

It has become common knowledge in our community that beavers have taken up residence in the swampy area between State Road and Cook Road. The beavers have been in this area for some time now and as I tell anybody that will listen, they have become so good at building their homes that now they even have help from other wild creatures. Beavers need a plentiful supply of water to keep them healthy and protected and it was while they were building their dam that I noticed the beavers were getting help from frogs. I watched the beavers slowly dam up the water and as the water began to rise, the frogs would tell the beavers just how deep it was by calling out "knee-deep, knee-deep" as the water backed up more and more from the beavers' dam! The amazing part of this whole operation was that when the dam was done and a large pond had formed, a large bull-frog would sit at the edge of the pond and warn anyone who approached the water by calling out "go-round, go-round"!!

Farming

John Fadden was visiting me and went to the barn with me to check on a new born calf. When he asked me if there was a danger the mother might sit on the new calf, I very thoroughly explained to him that after many prominent colleges, like Cornell, Canton A.T.C., etc., made exhaustive studies on animal behavior, they had reached a major decision. It was found that in research on horses, cows and various other animals, one very important fact was discovered. John immediately asked, "What was that?" I calmly informed him, "Cows don't sit!"

Dad and I were doing chores and he asked me to throw down five bales of hay for the night feeding. When I was up in the mow, I threw down the five bales, then I thought "Hell, I might as well throw down extra bales for morning." So as I let the sixth bale go, I noticed too late Dad already under the hole moving the bales. After he'd gotten up from under the bale I'd hit him with, he glared up at me in the mow and said "I send you to high school and you *still* can't count!"

Jack Carter was an old cattle dealer and farmer from way back. He was always very curious about how people were making out, especially farmers. I was visiting with some of my fellow firemen, when he stopped, mainly to say hello. When he found out I had bought the farm from Dad, he wanted to know how I was doing. He kept trying to find out how much my milk checks were. After two or three different attempts, he finally said, "Boy you must get some pretty big checks?" I replied to him, "Well they seem to fit in the mail box o.k."

Horseplay

We had bought a young mare, mainly to say we had a horse around the farm. We didn't use her much for work so she never really got broke into wearing a harness. On Saturday, Dad and us boys decided to hitch up the horse. After patching up the old harnesses left over from earlier days, we hooked her up to the cutter. Joe decided to be the first one to drive her. When he reassured Sonny he had complete control of the situation, Sonny let go of the horse. Horse, cutter and Joe were off like a flash, too fast, it seemed, for the aging harness! Half-way down the field, horse and cutter became separated! Pretty soon we were watching the horse walking behind the cutter as "we" pulled it back to the barn.

The next day Dad said, "I'll show you how to handle a

horse," and we proceeded to patch up the harness and hooked the horse up to the cutter again. When finally we had everything ready, Dad said, "Let her go. I'll take her into the deep snow. That should slow her down." He made sure he had a good tight grip on the reins and off they went, straight across the road into the field . . . that is the horse and Dad went into the field. It seemed that about an hour earlier the snowplow had gone by and left a fairly good snowbank in the entrance to the field. Dad shot across the road when the horse dashed over the snowbank, but the cutter didn't . . . it stuck solidly in the snow! With the harness being so old and ripe, it broke off the cutter, but Dad still had a good grip on the reins and he wasn't about to let go! He flew out of his seat, through the dash-board of the cutter and was dragging behind the horse in the deep snow . . . he wasn't going to let no horse get the best of him! He was giving a fairly good demonstration of what a gopher would look like burrowing through snow. Finally, after he had gone a considerable distance, he let go of the reins. As he stood up, we took the snow out of his glasses and hat. The horse circled around and went straight back to the barn, into her stall, and stood there as if to say "That was a nice outing, wasn't it?"

Skunk Oil

My parents must have wondered many times if they had made the right decision in having seven kids; the things that happened to us and to them would cause any person to get white hair. My father and mother were riding along our country road one evening and they came upon a freshly killed skunk on the side of the road. My father was always a strong believer in nature's cures and he quite often had to buy "skunk oil" when he wanted some. Finding this freshly killed skunk by the road, especially one that hadn't had its musk sac punctured, was a stroke of good fortune, or so it seemed at the time. My Dad carefully picked up the carcass and placed it in the trunk of the car. When they got home he decided to dress the skunk and at the same time remove the very delicate musk sac, hopefully without cutting a hole in it. It was not to be, despite my Dad's extreme caution in cleaning the animal. His knife slipped and punctured the sac. It doesn't take much imagination to figure out what happened after that. It wouldn't have been so bad if he had tried his operation out-doors, but because of the cold night he decided to do the job indoors. It didn't take long for the odor to completely saturate the whole house and whoever happened to be in it at the time. Naturally as my Dad started on the animal, we kids gathered around as close as possible so as not to miss a thing. We didn't. We got a full shot and God did it smell!! My mother was extremely anxious about us getting doused with the liquid. She immediately bundled us all into the car and straight to the doctor's office. One can imagine the welcome we got as we all trouped into the doctor's office . . . it was something like, "Get the hell out of here, I'll tell you right now no one will get sick from this except maybe me!"

More Bad Luck With Windows

As I've mentioned before, I admire my Dad's tremendous fortitude as he did his best to bring up his brood. One must marvel at the calm manner in which my father handled his discovery of a number of the barn windows peppered with numerous tiny holes! It was one of those boyhood games that escalated from pointing our "loaded finger" and hollering "bang, bang" to actually arming ourselves with real "live" ammunition. Granted the most powerful weapon we had was one "b.b. gun" and it was a test of strength and strategy to see who could overpower the person who supposedly had control of the much coveted "rifle". It seems, if my memory serves me right, the one who managed to successfully wrestle the b.b.-gun away from whoever had it, was actually in more "physical danger" than the others because with no actual weapon to use, we resorted to throwing hickory nuts, burdocks, small stones and finally somewhat larger stones (close to the size of an average golf ball!). The individual who had the "misfortune" of possessing the gun was under a constant barrage from the rest of the "combatants" as he dodged the projectiles flying his way! Luckily whoever had the b.b.-gun had enough smarts not to aim at anyone directly as he fired off a salvo of b.b.'s . . . it seems the same respect for the other person's safety was forgotten as we fired directly at the "owner of the gun" with our hand-thrown weapons (sticks, stones, whatever!). Anyway, in the course of the raging battle, our rather large barn seemed to come continuously under fire as different ones used its huge bulk for cover, sneakiness or possible prop for an "ambush". This was all well and good but in the efforts to flush out the "hidden combatants", whoever had possession of the b.b.-gun seemed to fire repeatedly at the barn!! Naturally the windows all jumped in the way of the on-coming b.b.'s . . . they wanted to join in the fun too, at least that was one of our alibis!

When the dust finally cleared, besides bumps, scrapes and a few bruises, all the combatants survived the battle some-what none the worse. Unfortunately, as we surveyed the "battle zone", the barn windows were one God-awful display of "peppered" panes of glass as b.b. after b.b. had passed through its thin glass! When my father discovered this strange phenomenon a few days later, his understanding of "kids will be kids" seemed to stand out very clearly as he remarked to my brother Joe, "the birds seemed to be getting pretty strong around here; they're pecking holes in the barn windows now!!"

A Warrior's Prayer

To his Creator he gives thanks for the deer, the beaver, the antelope and buffalo. . . . by their living and by their sacrifice, his family survives. . . . he gives thanks to their spirit!

To his Creator he gives thanks for the rivers and streams that flow providing his family and his animal brothers with the "drink of life" so vital for survival!

To his Creator he gives thanks for the plant life that provides food for the deer, antelope, beaver, buffalo and all the rest of Mother Earth's creatures; without them and the plants they eat, we would perish!

To his Creator he gives thanks for the air we breathe, the air we so preciously need to sustain life!

To his Creator he gives thanks for the blue sky; the beauty of a clear brilliant blue sky stirs the souls of all mankind. . . . this gift of the Creator's is one of beauty, serenity and peace!

To his Creator he gives thanks for the wisdom of truth, love, honor and respect for our Mother Earth and *all* her family!

To his Creator he gives thanks for Peace, though not all areas of our Mother Earth enjoy Peace; he gives thanks for those who know Peace, who work to preserve Peace and who invite their breather to come into their realm of love, Peace and truth!

To his Creator he gives thanks for the Spirit World where all of us, all of Mother Earth's Children, will dwell upon leaving the confines of this Earthly sphere!

To his Creator he gives thanks for the children who will inherit and take care of our Mother Earth!

To his Creator he gives thanks for our women who bear us children in His Likeness, our women who must endure the pains of giving birth, who must endure the sadness of her loved ones' hurts, who must endure the great loss of a loved-one's departure to the Spirit World, who must remain strong in their teachings and their wisdom!

David McDonald   215

To his Creator he gives thanks for our Parents and Elders who hold the knowledge of our Ancestors, who treasure with their lives the pride of being Indian, who guide us with love, faith and who show us the right path to follow!

To his Creator he gives thanks for our young men and women who struggle so hard to raise a family, who must constantly be on their guard to forever retain their Indian Pride, who must above all else remain true to their Indian Beliefs and Teachings!

To his Creator he gives thanks for making him in HIS Likeness. . . . for giving him a Soul to feel love, compassion and truth. . . . for giving him a mind to be able to *make* choices and most of all for preparing for him a home in the Spirit World where he will once again rejoin his family who have gone before him!

John Mohawk

John Mohawk is a resident of the Cattaraugus Indian Reservation near Buffalo. A lecturer in the field of American Studies at the State University of New York at Buffalo, he teaches Native American law and history. He has contributed to many Native American publications, including *Akwesasne Notes* and *Northeast Indian Quarterly*. With the Grand Council of the Iroquois Confederacy, he wrote and edited *A Basic Call to Consciousness: The Haudenosaunee Address to the Western World*, a landmark volume which has gone into many printings. Along with Oren Lyons, Audrey Shenandoah, Jacob Thomas, Tom Porter and a number of non-Indian scholars, he was one of the contributors to *Indian Roots of American Democracy*, a special issue of the *Northeast Indian Quarterly* exploring the influence of the Iroquois Great Law of Peace on the United States Constitution.

Origins of Iroquois Political Thought

When THE WHITE ROOTS OF PEACE was first published it became immediately apparent that the author had accomplished a pioneer work of sorts. Wallace exhibited astonishing insight when he alleged that prehistoric Iroquois had constructed a political philosophy based on rational thought. Not many writers on anthropology or oral history have found rational thought a prevalent theme among their subjects. Many professionals in this field operate on an expectation that rational thought is found only in the West.

Such cultural blindness is unfortunate because it automatically denies most of the academic and literary world access to the best thinking of many of the world's cultures. This unspoken doctrine helps to promote the tradition in the West that non-Western people are non-rational people. Wallace's work was an honest and commendable effort to go beyond that. He saw good rational thinking in a place where such thinking was not expected to exist and he promoted his discovery, almost breathlessly, to a disbelieving world.

Wallace saw good thinking among the people of the Haudenosaunee (as the Six Nations Iroquois call themselves) at a remote time in history and he took ownership of a small part of that tradition of thought. His insight was remarkable because although the Great Law of the Haudenosaunee had been translated and available for study for decades, it has been treated more as a historical curiosity than as a legitimate source of clear thinking political philosophy.

The political thought of the Haudenosaunee deserves to be judged on its own merits, not as an artifact of the past. We should investigate it today, question it, expand on it, learn from it just as we would from any doctrine of political thought. It will stand against that kind of scrutiny.

The story of the White Roots of Peace is the story of the thinking around the events which led to the founding of the League of the Haudenosaunee. The story begins among an Iroquoian-speaking people who then lived on the north shore of Lake Ontario, now located in eastern Ontario, Canada. According to the tradition, a male child was born under circumstances mysterious enough that a party of contemporary Iroquois to this day refuses to pronounce his name except during recitations of this story in ceremonial settings. They prefer to call him simply the Peacemaker. The story goes on to describe his early childhood and his eventual rejection by his own people. He was a young man when he crossed the lake to the land of the Mohawks specifically for the purpose of carrying his political philosophy.

Among the Mohawks this young man sought out the most frightening men, men who were known as assassins. It is here our story begins.

This was a time of great sorrow and terror for the Haudenosaunee. All order and safety had broken down completely and the rule of the headhunter dominated the culture. When a man or woman died, whether of accident or natural causes, their relatives hired a soothsayer who then interpreted the death as the result of the magical charms of a specific other. The aggrieved family then sought vengeance and a member set forth with the purpose of finding the unsuspecting and arguably innocent offender and exacting revenge. That killing sparked a spiral of vengeance and reprisal which found assassins stalking the northeastern woodlands in a never-ending senseless bloodletting.

The Peacemaker sought out the most remarkable survivors of this random and undeclared war and he initiated discussions with them. His exact words are lost to us now, but the essence of his approach is clear. He began discussion in the bark hut of a man who was about to cut up a victim for the dinner pot. It was in that environment he offered the idea that all human beings possess the power of rational thought and that in the belief in rational thought is to be found the power to create peace.

His words required considerable thought and understandably much discussion before his first student could take ownership of the ideas. He was not saying that human beings do not possess the potential for irrational thought. He was saying that all human beings do possess the potential for rational thought.

Unless we believe that all human beings possess rational thought, we are powerless to act in any way that will bring peace short of the absolute destruction of the other. We cannot negotiate with irrational human beings. In order to negotiate with other human beings, we must believe in their rational nature. We must believe they are not suicidal or homicidal by nature, that we can reason with them. Thus the first principle that will bring us the power to act is the confidence in the belief that all people are rational human beings and that we can take measures to reach accord with them.

We do not know the exact words the Peacemaker used to talk to the first of the Mohawk men he encountered. It took time. Perhaps days, weeks, months. His message was couched in a positive tone which reinforced the cultural messages with which his listener was familiar. The ministry of this remarkable man underlines the conviction – a major theme among the Haudenosaunee – that human beings possess minds and that minds give human beings the possibility of solving even the most difficult problems. In the area of negotiations between nations, the most desirable goal would be not only a cessation of violence but the active interactions which could create a better world for everyone.

The Peacemaker laid forth a promise of a hopeful future, a future in which there would be no wars, a future in which human beings would gather together to use their minds to create peace. He raised the idea of rational thinking to the status of a political principle. He promoted clear thinking as the highest human potential, and he preached it in the spiritual language of his contemporaries. The Forces of Life, he was saying, have given the human being the potential to use the Mind to create a better life through peace, power, and righteousness.

An important principle is that all human beings have the potential for rational thought. Another is that with a judicious application of rational thought a society could be created in which human beings can create governments dedicated to the proposition that no human being should abuse another.

In our modern English, the goal of the society which the Peacemaker envisioned was one in which human beings are loving and caring and interacting in a positive way on the emotional level and in which collective rational behavior and thinking are possible and desirable.

For this plan to work the Peacemaker was required to convince a very skeptical audience that all human beings really did possess the potential for rational thought, that when encouraged to use rational thought they would inevitably seek peace, and that the belief in the principles would lead to the organized enactment of the vision.

The test of this thinking is found in the converse of the argument. If you do not believe in the rational nature of the human being, you cannot believe that you can negotiate with him. If you do not believe that rational people ultimately desire peace, you cannot negotiate confidently with him toward goals you and he share. If you cannot negotiate with him, you are powerless to create peace. If you cannot organize around those beliefs, the principles cannot move from the minds of men into the actions of society.

The Peacemaker spent considerable time moving from individual to individual among the leadership of the peoples who much later would come to be known as the Mohawk, the Oneida, the Onondaga, the Cayuga, and the Seneca nations. His mission appears to have taken time. He was interested in reaching the thinking of each of these human beings as individuals. He seemed to go right at the intended target individual to offer his hope for the future of mankind, his definition of a way of coming to power, to peace, and to a better tomorrow for all his people, indeed for all mankind.

The story went on to relate that at this time an Onondaga leader, who was called Hiawatha, had quit Onondaga society in disgust and grief at the deaths of his beloved daughters. The Peacemaker learned of this man's plight and moved to join him in the forest.

The forest meeting between the Peacemaker and Hiawatha recounts a powerfully emotional transaction which took place at a small lake at a prehistoric time. The Peacemaker approached Hiawatha and extended an offer to pull from the older man the grief which had frozen his thinking and plunged him into despair. Speaking directly to Hiawatha's despair and hopelessness, the Peacemaker used soothing words and sincere care to wipe away the tears from his eyes and remove the lump from his throat. He unplugged the ears and restored Hiawatha to a whole man so that he could see, talk and use his mind.

The message in this transaction is a very important one which needs attention in the area of political theory. The Peacemaker and Hiawatha seem both conscious of the fact that human beings reach places of psychological pain, or feelings of rage, or despairing of hope. They recognized that at such times it is difficult to reach clear thinking and they directed a considerable amount of attention to the pain being felt.

In this particular instance, the pain Hiawatha felt at the death of his daughters has led him to despair of life. On the day the Peacemaker found him sitting beside the small lake, Hiawatha's mind was clouded in grief. By countering the grief, by showing care and a commitment to brotherhood, the Peacemaker brought Hiawatha from a place of despair, eventually to a place of hope.

This encounter has powerful implications in the cultural history of the Haudenosaunee. The historical incident at which the Peacemaker recruited Hiawatha provided the model for the condolence practices in the installation of leaders, and provided some of the process by which peace treaties were to be conducted in this part of the world for a long time.

The Peacemaker's effort was a process that brought a good message about human beings. Rather than dwelling upon negative images of the origins of the human spirit, the Peacemaker offered the suggestion that the human being is essentially a benign entity, possessing the power of rational thought. He has some powerful cultural assistance. The Haudenosaunee Creation Story, which we can assume predates the foundation of the League, is replete with symbols of a rational universe. In the Creation Story, the only creature with a potential for irrational thought is the human being. All the other creatures of Nature are natural, i.e. rational

Nature is depicted as a threatening and irrational aspect of existence in the West's cosmologies. The Haudenosaunee cosmology is quite different. It depicts the natural world as a rational existence while admitting that human beings possess an imperfect understanding of it. The idea that human beings have an imperfect understanding of the rational nature of existence is something of a caution to Haudenosaunee in their dealings with nature. Conversely, the idea that the natural world is disorganized and irrational has served as something of a permission in the West and may be the single cultural aspect which best explains the differences between these two societies' relationships to Nature.

The thinking behind the application of these kinds of principles has survived, though the exact words have not. What do you say to a fellow who has been on countless headhunting forays? How do you convince him that a society which has reached chaos can be turned into a society which provides safety and hope? How do you convince him that the thirst for revenge is the source of diminishment of his own human potential?

It takes a powerful personality using excellent thinking to do that. The Peacemaker was such a leader. He had to try to take each of the people he approached and to work with them until that person came to ownership of the ideas. He was powerful in the sense that he could demonstrate the principle of the power of the mind. He was able to explain the need for peace to people whose minds had been twisted by hate and terror.

The teachings of the Peacemaker were not slogans so much as a way of thinking. It was not possible to take action to bring about a solution of the blood feuds because people simply could not think clearly in an environment dominated by revenge and death, fear and hatred. The Peacemaker brought a process of clear thinking to that reality.

Many times in the process of telling about the ideas of the Great Peace one hears the admonition to "put your minds together as one mind," to think. All the things which are barriers to clear thinking, all the emotions which invade the process are ritually dusted off by the parties who participate. Every effort to achieve the clearest possible thinking is used. The Peace is based on the best and clearest thinking, the best rational thought of which men are capable.

The Peacemaker took this process from village to village and nation to nation throughout the country of the Haudenosaunee. He began with the Mohawks, among whom he found followers who looked like disciples. He lifted their spirits, inspired them, unified them, and then moved on to the Oneidas.

He promised them power. Not military power, but the power of righteousness. Where would this power of righteousness come from? In some societies it is a negative idea because righteousness is often presumptuous, unthinking, and uncaring. He defined righteousness as the result of the best thinking of collective minds operating from principles which assume that a sane world requires that we provide a safe environment for our children seven generations into the future.

The objective of the Peacemaker was a world safe from the irrational behavior of people caught in the grip of fear and hatred and conflict. He moved to enable the Haudenosaunee to provide the center of this new world. Onondaga would be the capital, the gathering place of this new and positive human energy. Thus would he plant a tree at Onondaga as a symbol of Peace. Under the limbs of that tree would gather the nations of the world.

So many writers of Haudenosaunee or colonial history stress the military power of the League. They try to portray the League as a military alliance, partly because they understand unity in those terms, and partly because they do not understand the true history. Every possible piece of evidence is cited to show that the League was an evil empire, that the Pax Iroquoia was the result of a cruel and dehumanizing imposition of military force on subject peoples.

The Haudenosaunee did not rule by force of arms but by the power of the mind. The Haudenosaunee were powerful all out of proportion to their numbers because they were able to manage complex alliances based on persuasive visions of reality which very large numbers of people shared.

Again and again in history we will hear that the Haudenosaunee (Iroquois) were great orators, persuasive, given to excellent expression of ideas. Logic was their major tool, a tool of survival. It is not mysterious that the Haudenosaunee were so powerful. It is not mysterious that they were surrounded by many potential enemies, outnumbered by the Algonkians, outnumbered by the other Iroquoians, and that they not only survived but prospered. Through most of the period of recorded history and in the tradition of pre-recorded history, Onondaga was a capital at which decisions affecting the continent were made.

The decisions made at Onondaga were more an outgrowth of the principles of the League which were encompassed in such documents as the Silver Covenant Chain, a treaty of friendship and mutual respect for sovereignty, the Two Row Wampum, and other legal documents serving the same purpose. True to the philosophy of the Peacemaker, Onondaga became important as a place at which thinking was done. The tree flourished for a long time. In the minds of contemporary Haudenosaunee, it continues to flourish.

The thinking which created the Four White Roots of Peace, which inspired the creation of the League of the Haudenosaunee, which laid the foundation for many of the principles of democracy now embraced by the West, is not obsolete thinking. When Europeans first arrived on the shores of North America they lacked the most rudimentary skills of survival. They could not prepare corn, could not hunt turkey, and were unprepared for winter. The Indians at that time had to teach them the skills of survival in the new world. Beyond the more mundane skills of survival, beyond the advantages found in the Indian agriculture and the Indian pharmacopoeia, the Europeans also encountered the Indian mind.

So much of the thinking of these Indians found its way into the European mind that the revolution of thought which separates the Medieval World from the Modern

World can be readily traced to the interaction between the Europeans and the natives of the Americas. It is rarely discussed. The European mind of 1600 or earlier was to our modern eyes a curious mixture of thoughtless faith and barbarous customs.

Europeans learned the custom of the bath in North America. They learned to think in egalitarian terms; they heard themselves repeating the heresies they heard from the Indians questioning doctrine of divine rights of kings. They began to adopt the Indian custom of democratic social ideals; they became healthy skeptics in the way that Indian people showed them healthy skepticism. This way of thinking was the most powerful change Europe experienced in the Americas. It was to change the face of Europe and the world forever.

There was however, another survival skill which was not completely transmitted. It was the survival skill of negotiating a truly peaceful settlement and the vision of a totally peaceful future. It is the survival skill we, who live in the late Twentieth Century, probably need the most.

The people of our time exist in a political atmosphere in which war has become obsolete, yet the effects of war are with us constantly. The Balance of Terror which exists and which at this writing has created 50,000 warheads with enough explosive power to destroy all complex life on the planet suggests that to survive we would need to apply our very best intelligence to the problem. What stands in our way today has many similarities to the forces which confronted the Peacemaker when he alighted from his canoe and sought the first Mohawk. What stands in our way is our basic belief that the other side is irrational and therefore we cannot negotiate. Our principal emotion around our potential for survival is fear. It invades our collective ability to think rationally, to invent new and comfortable ways to achieve the goal of peace.

A people living in fear cannot apply their potentially best thinking to solving their problems. A people living under terror can barely think at all. A people living in terror will conclude that power is at the barrel of a gun.

They will not believe in their own human potential to use their minds to become powerful because they do not believe in the other side's humanity. Because they refuse to believe in the other side's humanity, they cannot believe in their own, on their ability to become powerful human beings in the way the Peacemaker spoke of centuries ago. They must remain powerless, living in fear behind an arsenal of unprecedented potential for destruction, an arsenal which can never be large enough.

The weapons may change, the distinct situations may change, but warfare and human needs remain the same. Human beings, in order to function at their very best, need to believe in a future. To motivate them, they need a vision of that future which they can help to create. They need to believe they have the potential to do what must be done in order to reach that future, and they need to have a collective identity which supports them in doing that.

Long, long ago on the shores of Onondaga Lake a man proposed that peace was a possibility. It was as radical an idea at that time as it is now. He proposed justice could be achieved, and that there would be no true peace until justice was achieved. He proposed that because human beings are rational and have a potential to use their minds, these things are possible. His vision contained many principles, with what nearly amounted to a faith based on the process of thinking. His effort carried an obscure group of Indian peoples to the center of the world stage of history. It was a major building block which enabled the Haudenosaunee to become one of the most politically and philosophically influential peoples in history. The principles of thinking the Peacemaker offered then were offered in a way that the people who lived at that time could understand. He talked of roots and trees and eagles and leaves. These were the symbols of his time.

Wallace saw those symbols and translated the profound nature of the thinking behind those symbols to the people of our time. The ownership of the thinking which took place then and the generation of the thinking which needs to take place now are our job. When we follow the roots to their source, rational thinking is what we will find. The White Roots continue to represent a tradition of thinking about ourselves as a species, and the responsibility to use our minds that we will continue to survive and to create a good world for our children seven generations into the future.

Tim Johnson

Audrey Shenandoah

Hodinoñshoní; Onondágegá; Ogönde:ná. Iroquois (Six Nations); Onondaga Nation; Eel clan.

I grew up here; lived here all my life. My learning comes from living, and from the customs and traditions of the Longhouse. My tutors have been the Elders, both men and women, of the 12 Longhouses I have known in my time. Mother of ten, I am now at 28 grandchildren and still learning.

I have ever so much to be thankful for.

Goñwaianni

Eddy and his little brother Percy at my door
  so excited and such expressions
  in their eyes and on their faces
  of happy and wonder and good.

They've heard birds before – they hear them all the
    time
  they live in the woods
  on a hillside

But now it's early morning

The people noises of the day
  have not yet quite begun.

Inviting me outside
  they want to share with me this sound
  of birds singing in a new day.

How do I choose my favorite animal
For they are all my friends
Each gives his own gift
In his own way
I am anxious, even weary
Things are just not right
If I have not seen one
In many days
Squirrel, deer, rabbit, chipmunk

One time while riding home
Along the highway 17
My little grandson said
"Don't tell me 'look' everytime *you* see a deer
I'm looking to find my own."

All my brothers.
Some say "All my relations."
Skanondon, acknowledged Chief.
Ohgwaih, Hotahyoni, Deygeyu'gih:
We share the earth together,
The air, the water, the sun, and the moon.
We do not fear the storms
Of rain or thunder or lightning.
We know they come and renew the
Strength and power
Of the spirit
Within our bodies.
The power and strength which walk
Upon the earth,
All my brothers
All my relations.

Hato's Gift

The wondrous gift has arrived!

The whisper of snow swirling
   gently, gracefully down to earth
   like white feathers falling
   from an eagle
   high up near the Sky World.

The face of Elder Brother Sun
   now and then looks through
   the cloud mist
   and sees children's faces smiling,
   hears the sound of joyous laughter.

Anxious young eyes have watched and waited
   eager hearts beat happy that once again it comes
   just as they remember it to be.
   Hato's gift has come to pass.

Eyes beam bright and shiny
   remembering the feel of first snowflakes
   touching and melting on cheeks
   already rosy with the tingle
   of excitement—and the cold.

Expectations have once more been fulfilled
   as silver and white ribbons of ice
   line quiet streams and ponds,
   fluffy white down envelops branches
   and boughs
   of trees and bush alike.

Audrey Shenandoah   233

In the stillness known by our ancestors
   Hato moves into the seat of honor
   as the gift of winter
   slowly comes unwrapped.

Grandmother Moon

Early evening is liquid dark,
   creation reposes in respect
   while the night puts on her dress.

Now flowing into view are stars,
   countless numbers of stars,
   each moving and dancing in place.

Night's dark gown I'm seeing now
   decorated with sparkling fringes
   on her shawl.

The women of Ohkiwe dance just so.

Grandfathers of long ago, you
   who knew the language of the stars,
   I heard from you as a child
   that stars make music as they move
   across the sky and beyond!

My senses hum along.
   I feel my woman heart in tune
   with mystery,
   with night, with stars.

Moon rhythms, moon powers
   Moon pouring out light
   And life.

Carol Snow

Carol Snow is a native of the Allegany Indian Reservation in New York State. Her tribal affiliation is Seneca, one of the Six Nations of the Iroquois. She has two degrees in zoology: B.A., Syracuse University, New York; M.S., University of Wyoming.

Ms. Snow began drawing wildlife in pen and ink in 1966 while studying coyotes. In 1980 she began developing a mixed media technique using ink and acrylic paint. Her subject matter consists primarily of wildlife/Native American themes. In 1984 she began printmaking. Her specialty in this medium is the tuilegraph embossment.

Carol wrote and illustrated eleven reports on endangered and rare species for the U.S. Bureau of Land Management. She provided the drawings used for the bald eagle and golden eagle exhibits at Northwest Trek wildlife preserve in western Washington. She also drew illustrations for Point Defiance Zoo, Tacoma, WA. Three of her embossments are included in the Washington State Arts Commission's travelling exhibit of Native American art.

Carol Snow specializes in depicting animals, particularly wildlife. She has found that animals are not only friends and companions, but also teachers. She learned much from the coyotes she raised and from hawks she hunted with during the years she was a falconer. She also worked in the rehabilitation of injured raptors. From her experiences she learned that every animal has spiritual integrity and that on a spiritual level all beings are truly connected. Her present teachers are two lady cats, who provide companionship and supervision while she is working. One of them occasionally helps her improve her paintings.

Drumbeat

Listen. . . . . . .
There! Do you not hear them?
Come away from your overcrowded city
To a place of eagles
And then perhaps you will hear.
Be still this once;
Hold the yammering
of your jackhammer tongue.
Take your stainless steel hands
From the ears of your heart
And listen.
Or have you forgotten how?
They are there yet
Through these hundred centuries
And all your metal thunder
Has not silenced them.
The wind is messenger,
Heed the whispering spirit.
Now. . . . the drums still talk,
From the grizzly bear hills,
Across the antelope plains,
In the veins of your blood:
The heartbeat
Of the Mother Earth.

Metamorphosis

I think I am a dancer,
  a singer of songs,
  a story-teller.

I fly and swim,
  walk on four legs,
  slide through the grass on my belly.

I breathe through gills,
  through hollow fragile bone,
  shake feathers into place on my wings.

I roll in the dust,
  smooth my fur with raspy tongue,
  startle at unexpected sounds.

I walk upright,
  two-legged, a woman,
  warm and soft, strong and vulnerable.

I walk in silence,
  with laughter, with spoken word,
  with solitary tears, with open heart.

Carol Snow 237

The Winter Dreams of Bears

they say that bears sleep in winter . . .
they say that the heartbeat slows;
   the breath that is life only just
     flows in and out;
the rich blood creeps through arteries and veins
   like an ancient autumn river.
they say that bears sleep during the time of deep
   snow
and leave no track, no signature that says,
   "I was here;"
that you cannot hear bears
   when blizzards howl their icy way
     across the northern continents.
they say that bears are defined by the shape
   and color of fur and claws and what they eat,
     where they are found;
so measure weight and length,
   study food habits and say,
                  "this is a bear."
. . . . they are only partly right.

we know that Bears leave the forms They wear,
   leave them sheltered in caves and hollow hills.
we hear the Bears' voices disguised in winter's breath,
singing songs of knowledge, pure and clear
   as crystal,
unfettered by the needs of bodies,
   unshaped by physical desires.
we know Their chants of power in the sounds
   of ice cracking,
     of snowflakes drifting in the morning sky.
Medicine Bears walk through our winter dreams,

Their immortal eyes filled with Light
and when They look at us, oh,
    when They let us see Them,
Our hearts are filled with crystal knowledge,
    We know the truths of Ourselves.
Spirit Bears are the Great Healers,
    the Light in ursine shape,
clothed in fur where rainbows dance,
    clothed in clarity and perfect harmony.

they say that bears awaken in spring . . . . . .
We know that Bears never sleep.

Spirit Song

I shall cross the border quietly when my time comes,
an old, battle-scarred she-bear moving soundlessly
   across meadows where larkspur grows -
the grass will bend softly beneath my feet
   and spring back,
leaving no broken blade to show that I was there.
The wind in the trees will muffle the sound
   of my footsteps,
erase any careless tracks I may have left in the sand.
Any who think they see my shape silently walking
will see only long shadows cast by granite,
   by sandstone.
I may leave strands of hair caught on the tips
   of branches
but only nesting birds will know for sure that
   I am the source.
I will become deliberately invisible in the first light
   of day,
crossing the final physical boundary to become
   free again.
There will be no trace of me or who I was
   for a time,
save perhaps a fragment of mineralized bone,
a stone fetish left as a gift of love
   for the Earth,
perhaps a song never quite clearly audible.
You may hear my voice when a wolf sings the moon
   into the sky
and think I call your name in the sound
   of a river flowing.
Perhaps you will know that I see you through
   the hawk's eyes,

that I am the presence felt
                              but no longer tangible.
My form shall have gone past all recalling,
but my spirit shall dance in the morning sun
    and eagle's flight.
Disguised as the slightest breeze, I shall caress
    your cheek
and with quiet loving, touch the Earth,
    be again the Earth,
                              and All-That-Is.

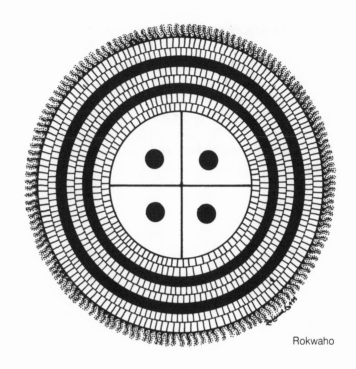

Rokwaho

Debra E. Stalk

Debra E. Stalk — Kawennanoron (Precious Word). Bear Clan, Kahnawake Mohawk, poetry, short stories, beadwork, leather work, traditional regalia.

"*Making Beadword, Remembering Life* is my first short story submitted for publication. It was written to express my gratitude and affection for my mother and grandmothers. It was also written for all people who have experienced the humor and closeness that comes from sharing such time with their relatives."

Making Beadwork, Remembering Life

I sat up all night doing beadwork with my mother. She told me all the stories of her youth and how her life was as intricate as the weave of the beads. She told me how Buba has made a swing for the kids and used her mother to test it. Grandma was sooo angry! Each story was a petal on a flower, or a leaf on the vine of her design. She would get up and laugh to boil some water for our tea, and then come back to sit down to bead some more. We were making a new dress for the social next month at the longhouse. She teased me that my dress had to be pretty enough to attract a husband. Once he saw my fine beadwork, how could he resist?! I smiled from under my hair which fell as I trimmed the edge of my skirt. I listened to her talk of when she was young and she and her mother sat to do beadwork. Only then it was little birds, beaded hearts that said, "Caughnawaga 1934,35,36,37 . . . ", or those little dolls in a 'papoose' that the tourists loved so much. Each bead was something to eat, and each finished piece meant work at the Indian Village the next day. Her beadwork then wasn't as leisurely as it is now.

We sat and talked about the ways I was learning now. I guess being an Indian in 1987 is different than how it was in 1941. Somehow it seemed easier then, everyone lived together in the same place . . . not spread out like now. She was proud that we could sit together and share the ways of our grandmothers. We talked about how good it was to be Ohnkwehonwe. To be able to share making beads together.

We gathered more material for my dress and "discussed" how it should be made. Of course, she knew but let me help so I wouldn't feel like *I* didn't know what I was doing (that was just her way of teaching me). I continued to bead afterwards – – one, two, three, four. . . . "What are you counting?", she asked. "Don't you know that only white man counts his beads? He needs to be exact because no matter how hard he tries, his work is still not Ohnkwehonwe. Whatever you make or do is and always will be Ohnkwehonwe--not 'Mohawk design' like they say in the museums."

We continued on and she told me stories of Doda who was blind and still did beadwork. My mother would lay the colors out and take Doda's hand to show where they were situated. Her designs and color combinations were always original because she had nothing to influence her.

I guess we were born with the gift of beadwork. Maybe it is inherent like eye color or teeth or something. Ma said it was given to us to teach patience. So everytime I was frustrated, I would bead. She would come home and ask what was wrong if I had a needle in my hand. I always had to smile when I did my beadwork!

Eventually I got better at what she taught me. I no longer oned, twoed, threed and foured. I would always watch her as she worked. One day, I giggled to myself because I heard her whisper under her breath, "enska, tekeni, asa, kaieiri, wisk". . . . and she looked up and laughed. Her eyes twinkled, and she said, "I was only counting the beads that fell off my needle, not the ones I put in my design – remember kheionah, Ohnkwehonwe – not made *like* 'Mohawk design'.

Niawen, Istah.

Kathryn Crowe

Amber Coverdale Sumrall

My writing is a continuous odyssey of discovery, exploration, connection, and healing. It centers me in the past, present, and future, sometimes simultaneously. I am the midwife and the woman giving birth. Each poem or story has its own unique process and form: I have learned to trust that no matter where the journey leads me, I will return with a clarification and wisdom I did not have before.

I grew up during the fifties, a time when people were shutting themselves down, swallowing their words and moving away from intuitive process and the natural world. My grandmother, Nellie June Coverdale taught me to trust my own small voice, to question, to challenge, to see, to listen, to honor the spirit in all things. In the morass of Catholicism and repression which surrounded me, her love and vision were unfailing beacons. She is my Muse.

My ancestry is Irish, Dutch and Mohawk. I live in the Santa Cruz mountains with hundreds of birds, wild mushrooms, flowers and native plants. I am a political activist, have worked for three years with the Sanctuary Movement. I am a disabled woman and teach workshops and lecture on disability issues.

I co-produce the women's reading series *In Celebration of the Muse*, now in its eighth year and am co-editor of the book by the same name, which features writing by 49 Santa Cruz women. My poetry and prose appears in *A Gathering of Spirit, Ikon, Sinister Wisdom, Akwekon, Passages North, Negative Capability, Women's Review of Books, With the Power of Each Breath, Toward Solomon's Mountain, Kalliope*, and other literary journals and anthologies.

*Upon entering this world the
Hopi were offered corn of various
colors by the Great Spirit, a
choice that would determine their
destiny. They chose blue, signifying
that although their life would be
difficult they would survive
all other tribes.*

Keams Canyon, Black Mesa

It is unwise to enter this place
without a spirit guide
a sense of what is sacred

Stretched between two worlds
I lie on red earth
reaching for sleep
the shaman's voice   insistent
rattles in my ear
hisses a strange language of warning

No rain falls here
radioactive tailings gouge
huge welts upon this land
already a graveyard for burned-out stars

I remember my grandmother's talismans
the gourds she carved and painted

with symbols of rain   thunderheads
bowls of special stones   an owl feather
her prayers to those who came before
her silent offerings of corn

On the edge of First Mesa
heat lightning arcs
bridging earth and sky
In volcanic craters   miles away
there is a stirring in ancient shrines

Constellations shift
petrified colors spin out across desert sand
Kachinas filter through boundaries of time
dance in fields of blue corn.

Pumpkin Woman

She creeps
   through umber fields
Belly-ripe she twines
   over and under me
      trailing fire

Vines tangle
Tendrils unfurl
Crowned with copper moon
   Pumpkin Woman glides
      into damp hollows
         steaming

Sighs hover
Lush furrows part
Pumpkin Woman dances
   songs in me
      and we sing
         rocking the autumn earth

Ceremonials

We beseech the earth mother
she has been in mourning
We call upon the goddess
she has been in exile
We call out to one another
we have been confused

In circles we gather
redwood groves
    sea caves
        meadow tipis

In moonlight
fires are kindled
    hands are joined
        legends honored

Our voices rise
chanting spells
    invoking grandmothers
        reclaiming ancient visions

We are sisters
We are witches
We are healers
    standing together
        weathering change
            forests of deep rooted trees

Infinity

The idea of infinity makes me crazy
I tell my grandmother
after Uncle Eugene dies,
his soul spirited away
like smoke on the Santa Ana winds.
She leads me to her bedroom
sits me at her dressing table:
a shrine of crystal candleholders,
silver urns, and music boxes.
She lights candles
arranges the half-circle of mirrors,
tells me to look into the glass.

In the shimmer of shadow and light
I gaze at reflection after reflection,
watch myself shrink
until I nearly vanish.
Time shifts like a dream
rolling slowly out of control.

Tahnahga

Tahnahga is a Mohawk woman born in Troy, New York. She attended the University of Wisconsin-Milwaukee where she finished her degree in Rehabilitation Counseling with an emphasis on chemical dependency and traditional healing methods for Native American people.

She has given numerous poetry readings throughout the Milwaukee, Wisconsin area. She has also worked with the Milwaukee ArtReach Board as a guest writer/speaker. Through her poetry/storytelling, she teaches Indian youth how to access their visions.

Tahnahga's writing reflects her Native American spirituality remembered through vision and dreaming. Her poetry searches for an understanding of the life cycles; through this she hopes to bring an awareness that Native American spirituality is alive and strong to meet the needs of the Seventh Generation.

Suburban Indian Pride

I remember

      Mom

On that blistering day
as the heat waves rose
from the black tarred highway
on our way back from the
Seminole Reservation
a full day of basketball
running and playing
you worried about me getting
ringworm in my barefeet
those days that Judy Jumper
and I shared as kids

Remember that day

        Mom

We saw the movie "Billy Jack"
It seemed half the Seminole Nation
was there
Judy Jumper and I saying
"Right on" – with fist in the air
"Those yellow belly white suckers
got what they deserved"
that day of awakening for Judy Jumper
and me

Remember what you said

        Mom

That day as we drove
to our white suburban home
fifty miles from the Reservation

    "Be proud that you are
    Indian, but be careful
    who you tell."

Giving Back

It is time,
 before the spring equinox to give back this lodge
 a time of rebirth
 a time to remember what was given by the ancient ones . . .
 remembering old wisdom, given through prayer and song . . .

Now i stand before you,
 your bones bleached as white as grandmother moon.
 in your nakedness, i remember your beauty.
 a young sapling peeled to expose your inner bark
 bending to form this lodge of woman's womb
 the beauty as you stood, a sacred place to come together . . .

Now i must take your frail bones,
 return them to mother earth
 these bones of time,
 battered by changing seasons,
 battered by a people who forgot the beauty of your lodge . . .
 this sacredness for which you were built,
 can we fully understand the depth of your soul.

Standing here,
 watching as the flames dance over your body,
 this giving back

I remember,
 the sacredness; which we came together
 as the smoke swirled above the cool summer wind
 a sacred fire, where tobacco offerings have been layed
 for a blessing within this lodge.
 This body made from willow who gave herself for
 the ongoing of the people.

I remember,
    what you said dear sister,
    the willow who gives her life is symbolic of our mothers womb . . .
    from within we are reborn, purified to receive this gift of light,
    power of all generations . . .
    within this darkness, our prayers are heard;
    beating hearts come as one.
    the Grandfathers hear our prayers,
    an eagle calls,
    as we felt his wings against our face, this healing power;
    we sang as we watched the coming of Blue Flame Woman.
    she dances, she swirls, she flies, for a moment we too are free.
    free from our humanness, together we dance,
    Blue Flame Woman has touched us all.

I will remember,
    always dear sister, the warmth and protection as we raised
    the flap of your womb,
    crawling on hands and knees, to greet the night sky
    of rebirth,
    this breath of life steam and wonder do we share.

I am crow . . . flying,
black shadow wings
gliding over this snowy
earth . . .
free from humankind
stepping in and out of time
to express myself. . . .
You see, I am person in
feathered black robe and
piercing eyes, which see
the truth in humankind.
I fly, calling out this winter day
to bring the chills of truth
back to humankind,
soul of the light hearted ones.
I am crow, trickster,
catching humans at their lies
bringing back the truth of time.
Watch as I fly, this crow
who changes form playing the
game of humankind.

Old Woman of Grey Hair

Old woman of grey hair,
eyes black as the night sky of grandmother moon
connecting our blood to this cycle of life . . .
cycle of truth . . . purification for generations to come
i seek your wisdom, this strong pulsating power of earth
that comes from within your inner soul.
this transforming power to greet my age,
of spirit who rises within me . . .

Old woman,
who am i, this indian woman?
who feels this burden of mother earth,
a people who walk with greed and selfishness of their
physical being.
why do i feel this age? one hundred, old woman am i to be you
this tomorrow?
what door have i walked through . . . to feel this pain of a people
who have lost inner self-truth

Old woman,
i sit across from the fire of this lodge, where women come with
moon to flow the rays of life for future generations.
here before i walked, smelled the burning sweet grass, sang the
ancient songs and shared in my womanhood of what was planned
seven generations ago,

Old woman,
i remember, as i stood in warriors garb,
my female body non-existing on this eastern shore,
black eyes piercing the invaders of this land, soul filled
with anger of this self-greed of people,
i feared the future, this future in which i stand,
a people who speak of new age.

Old woman,
what is new age?
those who seek old truth and knowledge,
the memories of a people
adjusted for convenience
destroy what they have sought

Old woman,
it is i, who sits in this lodge of time past
i watch as the fire dances within your eyes
of a child who was born with a cover of blue sky,
who brings beauty of life, strength for the people,
a child who walks in honor for the people,
mother earth feel these small steps this child takes
who will walk among the few who understand the song of creatic

Rokwaho / Daniel Thompson

Rokwaho, a.k.a. Dante, Daniel Thompson, born to a family of Mohawk artists and craftsmen at Akwesasne in November 1953. He grew up on the family farm and learned the agricultural tradition from his parents. From his father he learned carpentry and the craft of producing lacrosse sticks – now almost a lost art. Building on his agricultural background, Rokwaho became a student of Permaculture – a systemic approach to ecosystem care and management. From the age of nineteen, he has made his living alternately as a graphic artist, photographer and editor of various publications including Akwesasne Notes, The Rezz, Indian Time, and the Akwekon literary journal. Presently, Rokwaho is the literary editor for the Northeast Indian Quarterly, Cornell University. Fluent in both Mohawk and English, Rokwaho is experimenting with a new syllabic system of writing the Mohawk language. He writes poetry in both languages and has been published in anthologies, magazines, newspapers, and journals in North America and in Europe. Rokwaho resumed painting only recently and has begun to exhibit his paintings in shows around New York state. He is employed full time at CKON FM. He worked for two years as a Disk Jockey but has recently left the air to organize a news department for CKON and presently holds the position of News Director.

from Twoborn

Silent is the wood
and meadows green
The dipping paddles
of a two man
white stone dugout
carries a mile
in reflected stirrings
Onondaga Lake is painted
seamless and flawless
to the sky's even bowl

A smokey barren point
is the mark for
the white stone arrowhead
spreading wake far
to either shore
Unhurried paddles dipping
fan the fire smokier
an instant before
the arrowhead
pierces the mote
in the eye
of Onondaga Lake

Terror garrotes the air thin
and aswirl with magic currents
breathing the smoke round and
round and round
The approaching witch fire
whips skyward red and angry
in the dusk's airless smog
Heat fuming crooks the tangled
tending of the fire's keeper

The silenced paddles
bone-dry, writhe on the beach,
splitting and cracking and bleaching

Three painted faces
fire red in the witch glow
smile sincerely. . . .

Mongrel

Through a maze of spider webs
the land is barely perturbed
by the mongrel stalking

There is no tracking
the mongrel invisible
even to himself
reflected only in wind
and water flowing

But the land is empty
of tracks beyond the periphery . . .

Reflections diminish . . .

from Twoborn

Eye of the Loon

. . . a lake loon drowses and drifts
to mid water . . . in the premeditated
peace of a distant shining . . .
floating . . . bobbing . . . randomly
the bird flickers and blends
into a breathing pool
of reflected sunshine . . .
from the storystone
only the eye of the loon remains . . .
a glittering glassy jewel . . .
winking in the sun's
mirage . . .

. . . vagrant clouds blink
the lake's dancing glare . . .
a pearl vessel materializes
and dissolves between . . .
. . . and the eye of the loon
is a sparkle from its bow . . .

. . . my tongues perceive me
peculiar and disturbing rumours . . .
I would regard them not at all
were it not
so utterly unprecedented . . .

. . . rumours . . .

of Mohawks embracing

an alien mentor . . .
a preacher of peace and the great
silence . . . a would be prophet
of mine own doom . . .

. . . rumours . . .

of a white stone canoe
and an incident at Cohoes . . .
of Mohawks renouncing war
. . . breaking the age old covenant
of reciprocal vengeance . . .

. . . rumours . . .

and more rumours . . . mounting
like numbered days . . .
rumours . . . like the cold beads
of sweat upon my brow
swelling like a white water wave . . .

. . . rumours . . .

I would regard them
not at all . . . except

for the nightmares
of loons and singing mounds
dreams . . . real . . . as certain death . . .

. . . dreams . . .

of towering white pines
uprooted . . . become my enemies . . .
white scorching roots pursuing
like four writhing tentacles . . .
unavoidable . . . all engulfing . . .
. . . . .silence. . . . .

What would it be to trade
blow for blow . . . the Mohawks
behind the shield of their new
self proclaimed dispenser
of justice?

The Mohawks are closer
friends than foes of mine
in battle . . . we share
the dark power and the magic
of the Owl in our fury lust . . .
Would their new Cause
overpower their fearful respect
of Atataho?
My power can pierce only the veil
between transfixing terror
and a superstitious imagination
(preferably one that is battle
and journey weary . . .) and . . .
my rumoured legend to restrain
their clubs for that fatal instant
enough to make good my escape
from death and to bring them
to eternal silence . . .

. . . rumour . . .

is my insidious tool . . .
hooks upon which to fasten
the threads of magic . . .
to anchor my web of mystery
and to lure a curious supper to snare . . .

. . . rumour . . .

and what now is this? Do I
perceive my tool turned against me?
Why do I shudder and sweat
at the mere possibility
that these rumours could be true?

My power over Mohawks hinges
on their ignorance of mine own fear
of their relentless savagery . . .
The balance of power
is in the hands of a Huron!

. . . rumours . . .

and rumours only . . . until
a white stone canoe shores up
to my island and disembarks
some manner of paradox . . .
. . . flesh to rumour . . .

I have become without desire . . .
to move . . . or untwine
the grass that binds me . . .

How real He seems . . .
this realm of liquid veils
cannot eclipse His vision . . .

Mine own blood and water
have soaked down to unquenchable

depths of earth . . . my bones
bleach into stalagmite stone
formations . . . and blinking agates
stud my brittle contours . . .

How tall He seems above
the Great White Pine
He so gently uprooted . . .
I felt not a thread root snap . . .

My blood trickles past trout gills . . .
etching moon dance talismans
beneath the bottom beds . . .

He has gathered my weapons
and buried them with my robe
and bones beneath the roots of Pine . . .

I am become without desires . . .
a blinking agate rises
from root to pinecone
and glitters next
in the Eagle's twiceborn eyes . . .

Passenger Pigeon Poem

i dream

    still

of the

    magical

forests

    that

on a

    rain

heavy

    day

perched

    the

eagle

    within

reach

    of the

land

    of the

thunder

    people

i taste

    still

the haze

    scented

afternoon

    and the

feel

    of

nothing

    in

particular

    i want

to do

    until

hermit

    thrush

pipes

    of

heaven's

    visit

i am

    passenger

pigeon

Gail Tremblay

Gail Tremblay was born in Buffalo, NY in December of 1945 in a blizzard that covered the city with six feet of snow. She is Onondaga (Iroquois) and MicMac, French and English. Her grandfather used to tease her that she was the French and Indian War with her alliances mixed up, but she's always thought the Great Law of Peace of the Iroquois people was the only way worth choosing and still plants her Sisters, corn, squash, and beans everytime it starts to get warm. When she's not gardening, she teaches, makes art for contemporary galleries, and writes poems. Her artwork has shown internationally, and her poetry has appeared in *Northwest Review, Denver Quarterly, Calyx* and numerous other journals as well as anthologies like *A*

Nation Within, and *Anthology of Magazine Verse and Yearbook of American Poets.* She has two published collections of poetry, *Night Gives Woman the Word* (F Limited Gallery), and *Talking to the Grandfathers* (Annex 21, #3, The American Poetry Series, University of Nebraska-Omaha).

Drum

for Bill Blauvelt

Its ancient rhythms call us to our feet
and bid us move in circles on the earth
which, turning, circles round the sun
as surely as we move around the drum.
Drum, sacred circle, gift given by a tree
carved by human hands to make the hollow
form that resonates, fills space with steady
sounds of sticks pounded against skin,
gift of horned ones who chose to let the hunter
sacrifice their flesh. Two beings who lived
and grew embraced their death so music
could be born; their spirits feed the magic
caught in song. Transformation wakes us;
we know the voice that measures out the time
so we can dance. Patterns grow until they shape
the air, alter pulse and feed the breathing
brain. Drumbeat rattles bones inside the ear.
Vibration shakes the light; creation hears.

After the Invasion

On dark nights, the women cry together
washing their faces, the backs of their hands
with tears – talking to their grandmother, Moon,
about the way life got confused. Sorrow
comes through tunnels like the wind and wails
inside an empty womb. The need to be cherished,
to be touched by hands that hold sacred objects,
that play the drums and know the holy songs,
rises and moves as certain as the stars.
Women murmur about men who don't sing
when women grind the corn. There are too many
mysteries men learn to ignore; they drink together
and make lewd remarks – defeat makes them forget
to see the magic when women dance, the touch of foot
upon the earth that mothers them and bears
their bodies across the wide universe of sky.
Men brag how many touch them, who they use,
forget to help women whose love must feed
children that speak of fathers harder to hold
than distant mountains, fathers as inconstant
as the movement of the air. Mothers cook corn
and beans and dream of meat and fish to fill
the storage baskets and the pots. On dark nights,
the women whisper how they love, whisper
how they gave and give until they have no more –
the guilt of being empty breaks their hearts.
They weep for sisters who have learned to hate,
who have gone crazy and learned to hurt
the fragile web that makes the people whole.
Together, women struggle to remember how to live,
nurture one another, and pray that life will fill
their wombs, that men and women will come
to earth who know that breath is a sacred gift
before the rising sun and love can change
the world as sure as the magic in any steady song.

Sehià:rak

Always the memories come rising like smoke
from burning fields, from smoldering towns –
the soldiers whose grandfathers came from Europe
destroying hundred weights of corn, torching
storehouses of dry beans, orchards of nut trees,
fruit trees, and every longhouse they could find.
The sacred objects and household tools turn
to ash as the newcomers try to obliterate our words,
to write the history of a continent where no one
lived, a place they claim – they wish
even our ancestor's bones that make this ground
to become their heritage. They create myths
in which we disappear and make us study them
in school. Their teachers tell our children to be ashamed
of our old ones, our old ones who say:
"Thó nonkwá ionsasewe' tsi nisewaweiennó:ten."
"Sehià:rak nitesewehtahkwen."
They say our words sound funny, ridicule us
for thinking in ways they can not understand.
They report we are too much like our savage parents.
In boarding schools, they tell us, "Don't let
your people hold you back." And, "Earth
is no one's mother; we have dominion over it."
They tear and dig and destroy, build bigger
and more awesome instruments with which to kill.
Always the memories come rising like smoke
from deathcamps and bombed cities; it no longer
surprises us the world is mad; images
tear up the pages and speech grows raw.
The grief wells up in us and overwhelms
our tears. To forget is to become part of a lie;

to forget is impossible. Even the maggots
are part of the sacred circle, devouring the rot,
cleaning the earth; even the maggots can
teach us to survive. We struggle to grow,
to grow corn, to feed the people,
to keep the dream of peace alive.

Sehià:rak means: Remember it.
"Thó nonkwá ionsasewe' tsi nisewaweiennó:ten." means: That way
   go back   there to your culture.
Sehià:rak nitesewehtahkwen means: Remember it   your belief.

Gathering Basket Grass

for Mary Nelson

We stood in the muck on the edge
of Shoalwater Bay, the sun making
us sweat as we pulled up the grass
in bunches, triangular stems
popping as they were yanked loose
from the Earth which supports all life.
We bent and stood in rhythmic
motion thinking of our ancestors
plucking the ancestors of this grass
to make baskets, and as we dragged
the heavy bales up the rocks
to the road, we held the image
of the strength of grandmothers carrying
basket materials several miles home;
we held it in our minds. We threw grass
in the car trunk and drove up
the coast to wash off mud and sweat
in the surf before travelling inland.
Now, months have passed since I
sorted and stored these plants.
But every time I open the closet
the smell conjures an image,
I stand with two other Indian women,
my belly full of salmon, and harvest
the fiber used to keep the ancient art alive.

'Ohgi'we

Gifts of cloth and food are gathered; women meet
and name the night for feasting with the ancients
who've come before and by their loving handed
down the ways that make the nation constant
as the seasons of the year. The women send the men
to call the people in; the graveyard is restored,
the longhouse prepared to welcome the dead
who join relations to hear the words that come
before and remind us to be grateful for the patterns
of creation that make the circle whole. Tobacco
rises, is accepted by the spirits in the air. The dead
join with the living to dance around the drum
that sings when beaten as surely as the people
whose voices know the rhythm that makes motion
celebration shared by generations stretching back
beyond the memory of the ones who shape the sound;
men carry out the kettle while the people spiral
round. Outside, darkness hovers; moon journeys
across sky cold with winter coming; frost fills
the empty fields. Inside, the fires burn and warm
the spirits of old ones whose bones lay
like buried treasures in the earth rooting humans
to the dirt that supports their lives. Women call
their brothers to help hand out the food. The dead
feast with descendants who share the gifts
of gardens whose plants keep them alive. People
eat with ones so old no one remembers names
and with those whose loved ones mourn, the link
travelling in the blood of those just born
that binds them to lovers having children
before the great law came to earth and filled
the mind with peace. When the dead are full,

the dance resumes. The drummer plays the ancient
songs; ancestors remembering are glad some things
never change and whirl in stately steps timed
to the beat that vibrates to the corners of the room.
Before the first light, the women give bundles
of cloth, handing out gifts in memory of the ancients
who will go about well dressed; the dancers,
singers, cooks will make new shirts; the drum
receives a handkerchief; the drummer plays half the
     songs
again to make dance possible. The dead dance
and await the dawn. When first light comes,
the people prepare to raise up their arms,
and in procession, they follow the drum
outdoors where the dead can snatch scorched
cakes out of their hands seen by the rising sun,
a gift to keep ancestors fed for half the year. The
     living
careful not to fall so no one dies too soon, help
the dead to bear the cakes away; reverence
and love outlive the grave; these gifts care
for ghosts who, in their day, thought seven
generations that will come must feel the good
effects of what they did. The final song is sung;
the drum grows silent, gives up its skin;
the drumstick finds the fire, dissolves to ash.
The final words are spoken inside the room;
the dead are grateful; the living return home.

Roberta Hill Whiteman

Roberta Hill Whiteman grew up around Oneida and Green Bay, Wisconsin, earned a B.A. from the University of Wisconsin and an M.F.A. from the University of Montana. She has participated in several Poets-in-the-Schools Programs throughout the country, including Minnesota, Arizona, Wyoming, South Dakota, Oklahoma, Montana and Wisconsin. Her poems have appeared in anthologies and magazines, including *American Poetry Review, The Nation, North American Review, A Book of Women Poets from Antiquity to Now, Carriers of the Dream Wheel,* and *The Third Woman: Third World Women Writers in America.* A member of the Oneida Tribe, she has taught at Oneida, Wisconsin; Rosebud, South Dakota; and, most currently, the University of Wisconsin-Eau Claire. In 1980, she married Ernest Whiteman, an Arapaho Artist. Together, they have three children: Jacob, Heather and Melissa.

Star Quilt

These are notes to lightning in my bedroom.
A star forged from linen thread and patches.
Purple, yellow, red like diamond suckers, children

of the star gleam on sweaty nights. The quilt unfolds
against sheets, moving, warm clouds of Chinook.
It covers my cuts, my red birch clusters under pine.

Under it your mouth begins a legend,
and wide as the plain, I hope Wisconsin marshes
promise your caress. The candle locks

us in forest smells, your cheek tattered
by shadow. Sweetened by wings, my mothlike heart
flies nightly among geraniums.

We know of land that looks lonely,
but isn't, of beef with hides of velveteen,
of sorrow, an eddy in blood.

Star quilt, sewn from dawn light by fingers
of flint, take away those touches
meant for noisier skins,

anoint us with grass and twilight air,
so we may embrace, two bitter roots
pushing back into the dust.

In the Longhouse, Oneida Museum

House of five fires, you never raised me.
Those nights when the throat of the furnace
wheezed and rattled its regular death,
I wanted your wide door,

your mottled air of bark and working sunlight,
wanted your smokehole with its stars,
and your roof curving its singing mouth above me.
Here are the tiers once filled with sleepers,

and their low laughter measured harmony or strife.
Here I could wake amazed at winter,
my breath in the draft a chain of violets.
The house I left as a child now seems

a shell of sobs. Each year I dream it sinister
and dig in my heels to keep out the intruder
banging at the back door. My eyes burn
from cat urine under the basement stairs

and the hall reveals a nameless hunger,
as if without a history, I should always walk
the cluttered streets of this hapless continent.
Thinking it best I be wanderer,

I rode whatever river, ignoring every zigzag,
every spin. I've been a fragment, less than my name,
shaking in a solitary landscape,
like the last burnt leaf on an oak.

What autumn wind told me you'd be waiting?
House of five fires, they take you for a tomb,
but I know better. When desolation comes,
I'll hide your ridgepole in my spine

and melt into crow call, reminding my children
that spiders near your door
joined all the reddening blades of grass
without oil, hasp or uranium.

I'uni Kwi Athi? Hiatho.

White horses, tails high, rise from the cedar.
Smoke brings the fat crickets,
trembling breeze.
Find that holy place, a promise.
Embers glow like moon air.

I call you back from the grasses.
Wake me when sand pipers
fly. They fade,
and new sounds flutter. Cattails at sunrise.
Hair matted by sleep.

Sun on the meadow. Grey boughs lie tangled.
The ground I was born to
wants me to leave.
I've searched everywhere to tell you
my eyes are with the hazels.

Wind swells through fences, drones a flat ache for hours.
        At night, music would echo
from your womanless bedroom.
Far down those bleaching cliffs,
roses shed a torrent.

Will you brush my ear? An ice bear sometimes lumbers west.

Your life still gleams, the edge melting.
I never let you know.
You showed me and how under snow and darkness,
the grasses breathe for miles.

Dream of Rebirth

We stand on the edge of wounds, hugging canned meat,-

waiting for owls to come grind
nightsmell in our ears. Over fields,
darkness has been rumbling. Crows gather.
Our luxuries are hatred. Grief. Worn-out hands
carry the pale remains of forgotten murders.
If I could only lull or change this slow hunger,
this midnight swollen four hundred years.

Groping within us are cries yet unheard.
We are born with cobwebs in our mouths
bleeding with prophecies.
Yet within this interior, a spirit kindles
moonlight glittering deep into the sea.
These seeds take root in the hush
of dusk. Songs, a thin echo, heal the salted marsh,
and yield visions untrembling in our grip.

I dreamed an absolute silence birds had fled.
The sun, a meager hope, again was sacred.
We need to be purified by fury.
Once more eagles will restore our prayers.
We'll forget the strangeness of your pity.
Some will anoint the graves with pollen.
Some of us may wake unashamed.
Some will rise that clear morning like the swallows.

Ted C. Williams

The son of a Turtle Clan sachem chief and respected medicine man, Ted Williams grew up on the Tuscarora Indian Reservation near Niagara Falls, New York, in the 1930s and 1940s. In *The Reservation,* (Syracuse University Press) Williams recounts many of the old traditions that have since disappeared. There are vivid characterizations of unique tribal elders, stories of happy – and unhappy – family life, and a touching, yet hilarious, account of the Indians' efforts (led by the women) to sabotage a power project which threatened to destroy a large portion of the reservation. Williams writes of the land as life and identity for the whole tribe, of ceremonies – both ancient Iroquois and Christian – that highlight each year, and of the experience of leading the young men in their Midwinter Festival hunt. He tells what it is to be a Tuscarora.

The Trailers

DID YOU ever watch the purple grackles coming in from Ooskood-geh (the south) in the springtime? They fly along dragging those long tails with their heads twisting from side to side. Every once in a while they holler, "Khrih!" which, I don't understand all bird talk but later, you notice, they don't say so much.

They are looking for a nesting spot and they seem to be saying, "There's a pretty good spot! But there might be a better one just out of sight," because they always seem to keep on flying. In the springtime.

When the Tuscaroras first saw white people dragging their belongings across the countryside, they must of thought of the purple grackles because that is the name they gave them, Khree-hroo-hri(t) (looking-for-a-nest people) or purple-grackle people.

When the work on the Niagara Power Project began twenty-four hour twice around the clock activity, workers began drifting in from all over. Pretty soon uncles and buddies and cousins were coming in like purple grackles from Ohio and Pennsylvania to Florida. Of course, when they got there, they had to have a nest. The city of Niagara Falls, which half of is in Canada, just didn't have the room to hold all these flocks. Indians came in too, to do the steelwork and lots of them got rooms on our reservation. You can imagine what a wicked lacrosse team was formed. In fact, I don't think any Tuscaroras made the team. There were Indians from St. Regis, Caughnawaga, Manawaki, Oshweken—you name it, we had 'em. Two, from somewheres, were living upstairs in our house. And this was only the beginning.

This was only the beginning because when all the space from Niagara Falls to the reservation used up its living places, the white workers came onto the reservation dragging their trailers, looking for a place to put them. The chiefs held council. Maybe two or three councils.

Non-Indians are not supposed to live on the reservations and escape property taxes unless they are married to an Indian. Trailers, though, were excused in this time of need as being non-permanent living places. Also, laws are like the wind—who's to say if they are blowing or sucking? And you can't look at laws or winds like you can animals and vegetables. Also, the chiefs knew that the big wheels in charge of getting the power project done had enough pals in Washington or fat enough wallets to bend any laws towards their favor. Anyways, the chiefs said O.K. to the trailers—until the Power Project was over. Father was one of the first to register with the chiefs that he was having a trailer park. Maybe THE first, being as he was a chief too.

If a voice at Dog Street and Walmore had yelled "GOLD!" it couldn't have got more action. Overnight, the reservation had trailers coming out of its woodwork. Maybe at first the desperate trailer owners were ready to rough it. I mean, what is wrong with the childhood dream of camping in the wilds, living like first man and yet have a job nearby too? Well, for one thing, trailer owners have to poo too, and for just the three trailers which was the total of what we called our trailer park at our house, a third of our whole garden plot had to be made into a leach bed. Then of course, the bodies of the trailer owners were no different than ours; almost 100% water, with a need to keep 'em that way, and so our well went dry. By now, the reservation had electricity so THAT had to be octopussed out to the trailers too. Whatever else could be a problem, did, and however grateful the trailer owners were to find spots for their trailers, that vanished. For example, after about three years of this and no way of knowing how long the Power Project would go on, and with the leach bed full, Father found room in other trailer parks for his trailer people and ended his trailer park. I went with Father to the first trailer to tell them about this and the trailer man's wife started bawling. When Father said he had found a place for them, the man said to his wife, "Shut up honey, it's better than a jab in the ass with a sharp stick," but he moved the trailer out at night so as not to pay up the rent.

If we had problems with just three trailers, think of the problems of those with more trailers; and in numbers, trailers in trailer parks went all the way to a hundred or more. Somewhere along the way, sometime just before we gave up the trailer park ghost, the Tuscarora Nation decided that it ought to be collecting a small tax from each trailer. There may be nothing wrong with this except, Indians almost puke at the sound of the word TAX. That, plus Indians are scarey about demanding others to do something. And, being as, if you want reasons for monkeyed-upness, they're never that simple. For example, if someone asks me why I haven't been around to visit lately, I never say, "Because I don't like you all that much." I say, "I've been so busy." And speaking of liking, the chiefs, like any other leader-type people, are not the picture of angels in everybody's hearts. But what I mean is, supposing I'm greedy. That may be why I didn't visit Tom; because Dick and Harry had a big barn to play in or a basketball hoop on their house. If Tom says, "You never come to MY house," we could get into an argument because I'll fight back to keep Tom from making me feel guilty about my greediness. And NEVER will the word GREEDY or GUILT be used. We'll argue over little things: "You cheat at marbles!" "I do not!" "You do too!" "I do NOT!" So some of the REAL feelings on the reservation are held back until fists fly. Or bullets. Or court fees. So I think it's fair to say that probably the chiefs had trouble collecting this tax fee. Probably some paid while others didn't.

The reservation, as a group of – say – one thousand people, is no different than any group of one thousand people. Whatever fears, or loves, or likes, or dislikes, or prejudices, or religious beliefs, or jealousies, or the little flocking togethers of birds-of-a-feather, or whatever it is that MAKES people split into groups – those same things cause splits within the reservation. Maybe Indians are THE most splittable people. Our land has been split. Our tribes have been split. Our culture split. Our beliefs split. Our laws split. Our thoughts and hope and decisions, then, have a nice long history of forks in the road. Some of the non-Indian roads have brought gladness and some have brought a crushing of hope. So there's lots of distrust. I used to hide behind a tree when someone came to our house.

My little groups that I was split into was, first, the people living in our house. I trusted them. And trees. Also dogs and cats and chickens that lived at our house. Next came cousins my age and neighbors my age and some wild animals like rabbits. Next came older friends of my father and mother, and sometimes their dogs. Close to them came older cousins and neighbors and their chickens and some of their dogs. (Especially dogs that didn't bark and wagged their tails a lot.) Next came other relatives and frogs and any children on the reservation my age who were friendly. Next came any dogs or cats on the reservation that were friendly. Also, even before this, I liked birds but they didn't like me or my slingshot. Next came some Baptists if they were friendly and friendlier people that were not Baptist; maybe Presbyterian or Catholic or nothing. Also animals like woodchucks. Next came Indians that I didn't know very well but that smiled at me. Also toads and snakes. After that, I was pretty scary of people and animals that bit, like raccoons. I hid on black people or white people that came for medicine. Or strange Indians from other reservations. Or people with Canadian license plates on their car. Or anyone in any kind of uniform. And skunks. I hated loud or mean people from anywhere. Or dogs that bit or cats that scratched. And airplanes. For them, I ran and hid under my bed. I was born on the reservation and if all the others born there had many of these distrusts plus any that I didn't have, then there might not be too much trust all around, huh? And that just covers distrust and some prejudices that I didn't even know I was learning. What about if I envied something some other kid had? Oh you can make a longer list but not me. I might get to disliking myself.

So now here is a reservation with lots of trailer parks on it. Some were neat and clean with each trailer having its own yard. Others were crowded and had muddy or rutted driveways and parking places. Some had weeping leach beds and stunk.

Many Indians didn't have a trailer park. For some, it was because of the lack of money or land space to start one. Others didn't think it took any money to start one and let trailers park anywheres. Some that had land but no money said that they didn't want trailers; that it was wrong in the first place. Some said it honestly. Some had both land and money but were against trailers. Or didn't have the time or ambition. Probably a lot of owners were without business sense too and had problems collecting rent. Some, though, just plain saw the whole thing as a cluttering up of the reservation. Others went about their business not caring and not saying anything.

As work on the Niagara Power Project straggled towards an ending, the trailers did not leave the reservation in great numbers. Nobody could say, "On this one particular day, all the work on all of the project will end. On that day, all trailers must leave the reservation." Also, now, some of the white owners had left and had sold their trailers to Tuscaroras who were now calling the trailer their home. The chiefs began trying to sort out some kind of ending of trailer parks to go along with the ending of the Power Project and if they expected that it may not be a happy ending, they were right. Maybe Degonawida and Hiawatha (Hi-Ye(t)-WA-the(t)) had trouble forming the Iroquois Confederacy but I'm sure neither one of them would have said, "O.K.," if, after forming the Iroquois, they had been asked, "Now that you're done with that, how about straightening out the trailer court thing at Tuscarora?" That is, the reservation is really a very peaceful place most of the time. But in every house one can expect to find anywhere from two to eight, maybe ten (according to size of family) rifles and shotguns. These are for hunting. So go ahead and poke a very peaceful hornet's nest and see what happens. See what kind of open season gets declared.

Yes, there are many splits among the Indian people on the reservation — clans, religious beliefs, you name it. But for anybody that isn't an Indian and never lived like an Indian, that person NEVER EVER could understand what the Indians will fight for. I may not be able to tell about it exactly, but I'll try. I'll use myself for an example. I'll use myself and cats because I saw this thing in cats first. It seems that however deep a living thing is shown or given freely of love and kindness and freedom and peace and quiet and food and laughter – just plain good, good, good feeling – THAT whole feeling gets into that living thing's guts. And BOY! does that living thing like it. That is LIFE to that living thing and it wants to dish out that same feeling to everything – living or dead, that is around it. And so PRECIOUS is this feeling to this living thing, that it also develops the same depth of OPPOSITENESS to protect the precious "good feeling." Also, if it has had terrific freedom, it will also be terrifically brave; RECKLESSLY brave.

One night, in the middle of the night, I came out of a deep sleep because of this noise, "gaaaags – gaaaaags – gaaaaags." There was a little moon because in the dimness of the window I saw something moving. In my sleepy eyes it looked like somebody's head. In my sleepy ears I thought somebody was ripping the window screens to break into my room. Now here was a living thing disturbing my peacefulness. Instantly, I was ready to kill. What it turned out to be, it turned out to be my young pet cat. It slept in bed with me and my dog. What it had done, it had shit on my bed and was trying to cover it up. That's what the noise was. What gave it away was the smell. Up until that moment, my cat and I were great to each other. Now, though, I punched it against the wall. In its young life, it had had all kinds of freedom, so it was very brave. It attacked me tooth and nail. I went crazy wild. I had had freedom too and was brave too and to have my peace disturbed this badly, I went wild too and threw the cat right through the screening of my second-story window. At first I didn't know that its claws had ripped through my veins and blood was going all over my bed and everything in the dark. So, for a week straight, I stoned that young cat away from the house. In one week, so badly did that cat want the good feeling of life that it had before, that it got skinny and shaky and scary. I forgave it after a week but being as it was a young cat and not done growing, it was too late. It hissed and ran, hissed and ran. Then a dog chased it and caught it and killed it. I got myself a new kitten.

This time I wasn't going to let that happen again, so I loved it and fed it no matter WHAT it might do on my bed. It was a model T cat (brown with black stripes) just like the other one and in time, it grew up. Except the new cat had an extra good life. Extra freedom. One day that same dog that killed the other cat came charging after the new cat. What do you think it did? Nothing. At first, it just watched the dog come and then it jumped right on the dog's back and began tearing its eyes and ears to smithereens. It rode the yelping dog about twenty yards before it fell off and began washing up.

I think every Indian is like that. Because every Indian house that every Indian visits, and everything in that house, gives off that good and kind and precious feeling but don't – and I mean DON'T! – disturb that feeling. If you GO in with that good feeling the house will feel it too, and pretty soon the whole house will want to give you everything it's got and you will want to give everything that you have too. And you won't see any fences nor will you ever put any up. You'll eat cornbread fried in butter in any house and when somebody brings that same feeling to your house, your house will turn itself inside out for them. It can't be helped. That's the way it is. I know. Because when something disturbs my peace, I might as well go looking for a job poking hornets' nests because I'll be perfectly suited for that.

So. What happened with the trailer park thing? Along with however many groups or factions or splits there may be on the reservation, the trailer thing caused one more. Often a split causes all other cracks or differences to, for the time being anyways, heal up or patch up. Then the reservation becomes two main bodies. Well, three. Some didn't care at all. But here is a strange thing. Of the people that did not give one hoot one way or the other, some of these can cause a split. And that's just about what happened here.

The trailer park owners, as a group, put up a fight for whatever rights they felt they had. So on one side, there was the park owners and certain friends and relatives plus the people in the trailers themselves. There had to be people in some of these trailers who had made good, fast, strong friendships with the park owners. This alone might make some park owners go to bat for someone they liked. Also, probably the money that the friends paid for trailer space had become pretty good friends of the park owners too. On the other side of the split were the Indians who complained to the chiefs about the trailers staying on past the work on the project. Also certain ones among THEIR friends and relatives, plus now, the chiefs and THEIR backers-uppers. Maybe even some Tuscaroras now living in trailers. What is tricky, now, is that WITHOUT the people that didn't give a hoot, I don't think there would have even been a thing called "the trailer thing." Not even a real split. That is, a smoother thing would have taken place between the park owners and the chiefs but before that could happen, out of the group of don't-really-carers came the instigators. Young people. Full of fun and mischief. My schoolmates and I were always getting each other into scraps as a form of entertainment. Just as a tree can make a million matches, a match can burn a million trees and it just takes a tiny spark to start a fire. Like a kid saying to a grumpy trailer owner, "NYEAH-NYEAH, NYEAH-NYEAH, you gotta MOO-ove, you gotta MOO-ove." Especially if it's sort of "sung," over and over. That's the little spark, and a grump will always fan it, much to the joy of the singer.

There are numbers of ways of how the "fire" got going but it's easy to see that once hecklers got under the skins of trailer owners, and that gets passed on to the park owner (" . . . and what are you going to do about it?") then something could happen. Then the little heckler tells mommy and pretty soon mommy tells the chiefs. However it started, it came to a point where guns came out. On both sides. One park owner's house still has bullet holes in it. The protest and fight against the New York State Power Authority over Indian land was still inside of many people's skin and the protest against the trailers became powerful. A twenty-four-hour encampment of protest was even set up. Bullets are not the most symbolic sight or sound of welcome, especially during the moments when they are measured in feet per second and many trailers did not wait for any court order which can be measured in weeks instead of feet per second. It did come, though – the court order – and the trailers left.

So now the "trailer thing" is just a dot of reservation history because between the splits and cracks and healings – something – maybe right this minute – is monkey farting with that precious gut want of the Indians on the reservation for that terrific goodness-kindness-no-fence feeling; where the only loud noise is laughter. Flies, though, fall into ointments all the time.

Acknowledgements

All of the work in this anthology is printed with the permission of the original authors. Copyright remains in their names and permissions to reprint should be requested of the authors. Some of the poems and prose pieces appeared previously in the following publications:

Salli Benedict: "The Tsioneskwenrie Plant People" in *American Indian Culture and Research Journal*, 7:2, 1983. "Tahatohontanekentseratkeronakwenhakie" in *Earth Power Coming* edited by Simon Ortiz, Navajo Community College Press. "Sweetgrass is Around Her" in *A Gathering of Spirit* edited by Beth Brant, Sinister Wisdom Books.

Peter Blue Cloud: "Winter Crow" first appeared in *Akwekon*. All other selections first published in *The Greenfield Review*.

Ateronhiatakon/Francis Boots: "Iroquoian Use of Wampum" in *The Quarterly*, St. Lawrence County Historical Association, January 1968.

Beth Brant: "Indian Giver" and "Daddy" in *Mohawk Trail*, Firebrand Books.

Katsi Cook: "The Woman's Dance" and "Womans' Thread" in *Northeast Indian Quarterly*.

Melanie Ellis: "Ode: to an Indian Artist" in *Akwekon*.

Ray Fadden / Tehanetorens: "Needles" in *Northeast Indian Quarterly*. "Migration of the Iroquois" in *Tales of the Iroquois*, Volume II, Akwesasne Notes. "The Gift of the Great Spirit" in *Tales of the Iroquois*, Akwesasne Notes.

Richard Hill: all selections from *Skywalkers: A History of Indian Ironworkers*, Woodland Indian Cultural Center, Brantford, Ontario.

Karoniaktatie / Alex Jacobs: "The Politics of Primitivism" in *Akwekon*.

Maurice Kenny: "Passions" in *River Styx*. "Going Home," and "Legacy" in *Between Two Rivers: Selected Poems 1956–1984*, White Pine Press. "Yaikni" in *Earth Power Coming* edited by Simon Ortiz.

Bruce King: two untitled poems in *The Clouds Threw This Light*, Institute of American Indian Arts Press. "A Contemporary Chant to the Great Spirit" in *Turtle Quarterly*.

Oren Lyons: "Power of the Good Mind," and "Water is a Sacred Trust" in *Daybreak* Magazine.

David McDonald: "The Beavers and Frogs" in *Indian Time*. "Skunk Oil" and "Horseplay" in *Northeast Indian Quarterly*.

John Mohawk: "Origins of Iroquois Political Thought" was the Introduction for The Chauncy Press edition of *The White Roots of Peace* by Paul Wallace. This abridged version appeared in *Northeast Indian Quarterly*.

Carol Snow: "Drumbeat," and "Metamorphosis," in *Akwekon*.

Amber Coverdale Sumrall: "Ceremonials" in *Woman Spirit*. "Infinity" in *Passages North*. "Pumpkin Woman" in *Akwekon*.

Daniel Thompson / Rokwaho: "Mongrel," and "Eye of the Loon" in *Akwekon*. "Passenger Pigeon Poem" in *Wounds Beneath the Flesh*, White Pine Press.

Roberta Hill Whiteman: *Star Quilt*, Holy Cow! Press.

Ted C. Williams: "The Trailers" in *The Reservation*, (Syracuse: Syracuse University Press, 1976), pp. 205–213. By permission of the publisher.